WOMEN PSYCHOTHERAPISTS

WOMEN PSYCHOTHERAPISTS

Journeys in Healing

EDITED BY
LILLIAN COMAS-DÍAZ, PHD
MARCELLA BAKUR WEINER, PHD

JASON ARONSON
Lanham • Boulder • New York • Toronto • Plymouth, UK

Published by Jason Aronson
A wholly owned subsidiary of The Rowman & Littlefield Publishing Group, Inc.
4501 Forbes Boulevard, Suite 200, Lanham, Maryland 20706
http://www.rowmanlittlefield.com

Estover Road, Plymouth PL6 7PY, United Kingdom

British Library Cataloguing in Publication Information Available

Library of Congress Cataloging-in-Publication Data

Women psychotherapists : journeys in healing / edited by Lillian Comas-Díaz, Marcella Bakur Weiner.
p. cm.
Includes bibliographical references and index.
ISBN 978-0-7657-0787-1 (cloth : alk. paper) — ISBN 978-0-7657-0789-5 (ebook)
1. Psychotherapy—Biography. 2. Women—Biography. I. Comas-Díaz, Lillian. II. Weiner, Marcella Bakur, 1925–.
[DNLM: 1. Psychotherapy—Autobiography. 2. Women—Autobiography. WZ 150]
RC475.W66 2011
616.89'14082—dc23 2011012722

™ The paper used in this publication meets the minimum requirements of American National Standard for Information Sciences—Permanence of Paper for Printed Library Materials, ANSI/NISO Z39.48-1992.

Printed in the United States of America

For wisewomen from the past, present, and future.
—Lillian Comas-Díaz

For my sisters, Dora and Lillian, my models for femininity at its purest.
—Marcella Bakur Weiner

CONTENTS

Acknowledgments

Our journey from women psychotherapists to female healers inspired us to develop this book. The completion of this anthology renewed our commitment to healing from a female perspective. Moreover, it strengthened our sisterhood. We would like to express our deep appreciation to the women psychotherapists who shared their stories with us. These contributors are female healers who infused this book with passion, compassion, and wisdom. Additionally, we would like to thank our Jason Aronson editors, Julie Kirsch and Samantha Kirk, for their assistance in the completion of this book. Our life partners, Frederick M. Jacobsen (Lillian's husband) and Wilhelm Weiner (Marcella's husband) provided us with constant support and love during the gestation and birth of this volume. Last, but not least, we would like to acknowledge our female clients—girls, adolescents, and women who graciously invited us into their hearts.

Introduction
Wisewomen—The Evolution of Female Psychotherapists

LILLIAN COMAS-DÍAZ AND MARCELLA BAKUR WEINER

WOMEN HAVE AN INHERENT PREDISPOSITION for healing. Their relational abilities and their caretaking roles foster females' healing capacities. For instance, research has documented the salutary effect of having a sister. A large study examining families with at least two children found that having a sister protected females from being lonely, depressed, guilty, unloved, self-conscious, and fearful (Padilla-Walker, et al., 2010). The study researchers concluded that sisters tend to be better listeners, better at talking out problems, and take on the caretaker role better than brothers (Padilla-Walker, et al., 2010). Besides their socialization to become caretakers, women embody a tending instinct. A kind of female relaxation response, the tending instinct facilitates the release of oxitocin, an antistress neurohormone (Taylor, 2002). Certainly, such female physiological response enhances women's healing abilities. In other words, females have the capacity to nurture others and thus, they tend to promote a sense of well-being. These attributes enable women to become skilled as healers.

Women have been healers since the dawn of time (Brooke, 1995). Known as wisewomen, these healers acted as shamans, herbalists, priestesses, sorceresses, conjurers, psychics, prophetesses, diviners, midwives, abortionists, and in many other healing roles. In *Witches, Midwives and Nurses: A History of Women Healers*, Barbara Ehrenreich and Deirdre English (1973) described how men co-opted the healing profession as practiced by such wisewomen from the earlier times, and consequently alienated, persecuted, and subjugated female healers with the rise of the male-dominated medical profession.

Today, wisewomen are recovering their voices and reclaiming their healing legacy. Many women channel their innate ability to nurture, empower, and heal through their role as psychotherapists. Indeed, most of the psychotherapists and their clients are females. The feminization of psychotherapy denotes the transformative effect of the female presence in psychotherapy resulting from a dramatic increase in women practitioners as well as a decline of incoming number of male therapists (Philipson, 1993).

What makes a woman become a psychotherapist? What is the process of conducting psychotherapy from a female perspective? Is there a developmental passage from becoming a woman psychotherapist to evolving as a female healer? This unique anthology attempts to clarify these questions by illuminating women's journey from psychotherapist to healer.

The professional literature has paid some attention to the topic of becoming a psychotherapist (Goldfried, 2000; Farber & Norcross, 2005; Shay & Wheelis, 2000). However, the stories of women psychotherapists still remain rarely told. Although few publications have addressed psychotherapists' gender and cultural background in their development (Greene & Brodbar, 2010; Kaslow & Kelly, 2010), these narrations have not focused on the interaction of gender, ethnicity, race, culture, age, sexual orientation, religion, and disability with the maturation of female healing capacities. *Women psychotherapists: Journeys in Healing* attempts to fill this gap.

To accomplish this goal, we invited seasoned female psychotherapists to address the professional and personal issues in their development as a healer. We asked our contributors to narrate their story in their own voice and to use creativity in their storytelling. You will meet 11 remarkable women in this anthology. These wisewomen are accomplished psychotherapists as well as gifted healers. Trained in psychology, psychiatry, and clinical social work, our contributors represent diverse theoretical orientations including psychodynamic, cognitive behavioral, experiential, Jungian, feminist, multicultural, systems, family, and integrative psychotherapies. Ranging in age from 37 to 83 years, these wisewomen come from all walks of life. They are White, African American, Latina, mixed race, and Indian women who endorse Christian, Jewish, Buddhist, and Hindi religions or none. Many of them subscribe to a syncretistic spirituality.

Our contributors share professional and personal journeys that culminate in achieving an identity as a female psychotherapist-healer. As you meet these wisewomen, you will become familiar with how their life experiences shape their healing journey. Specifically, you will find how they chose, or in some cases, were chosen, to become psychotherapist-healers.

Moreover, you will learn how they combine their mind and heart into their healing profession.

In collecting these women's stories, we wondered how their life circumstances interact with their professional development. In other words, we were interested in how their gender and culture interaction inform how they practice psychotherapy. To facilitate the unfolding of their narratives, we offered our contributors a guide. We suggested that they share their experiences of becoming a woman psychotherapist, of being a female psychotherapist, and of their female healing experience. Moreover, we asked them to offer theoretical, conceptual, and practical implications to other women therapists as well as to those women who are considering becoming psychotherapists. Specifically, we asked the psychotherapist-healers to provide lessons learned throughout their journeys. In particular, we asked them to offer recommendations to women who are psychotherapists or are considering becoming one.

You will find in this book a *herstory* filled with lessons of wisdom, resilience, and hope. The wisewomen in this collection regale you with insights and reflections about womanhood, healing, and life. Their stories offer encouragement, strength, and inspiration. Perhaps you recognize yourself in these women's portraits. You may identify with their struggles as well as with their triumphs. As you learn from these psychotherapists-healers' wisdom, you may find truths that you think you did not know. Likewise, you may remember *forgotten* lessons. Through this process you may develop and deepen a connection to your inherent healing ability. As you meet these extraordinary women, you may accept an invitation to join a special sisterhood. The only membership requirement is your willingness to heal with passion and compassion. These women's stories offer you this blessing: "May your heart guide you into a healing path."

References

Brooke, E. (1995). *Women healers: Portraits of herbalists, physicians and midwives.* Rochester, Vermont: Healing Arts Press.

Ehrenreich, B., & English, D. (1973). *Witches, midwives and nurses: A history of women healers.* Old Westbury, New York: The Feminist Press.

Farber, B., & Norcross, J., eds. (2005). Why I (really) became a psychotherapist. (special issue), *In Session, 61*(8), 943–1031.

Goldfried, M., ed. (2000). *How therapists change: Personal and professional reflections.* Washington, DC: American Psychological Association.

Greene, B., & Brodbar, D., guest editors. (2010). A Minyan of women: Family dynamics, Jewish identity and psychotherapy practice. *Women & Therapy*, *33*(3–4), 153–485.

Kaslow, N., & Kelly, J., eds. (2010). The diversity status of the psychotherapist. *Psychotherapy, Theory, Research, Practice, Training* (special section), *47*(2), 143–197.

Padilla-Walker, L., Harper, J., & Jensen, A. (2010). Self-regulation as a mediator between sibling relationship quality and early adolescents' positive and negative outcomes. *Journal of Family Psychology*, *21*(4), 419–428.

Philipson, I. J. (1993). *On the shoulders of women: The feminization of psychotherapy.* New York: Guilford Press.

Shay, J. J., & Wheelis, J., eds. (2000). *Odysseys in psychotherapy*. New York: Ardent Media, Inc.

Taylor, S. E. (2002). *The tending instinct: How nurturing is essential to who we are and how we live.* New York: Holt.

The Birthing of a Womanist Psychologist
On Becoming a Guide to Healing and Empowerment

1

THEMA BRYANT-DAVIS

I AM A WOMAN, A WOMAN OF AFRICAN DESCENT. I am a woman of African descent living in America. These three aspects of my identity and the ways I was socialized into a sacred understanding of what it means to be an African American woman have all shaped my decision to focus my life on healing and empowerment. I am a psychologist who works primarily with trauma survivors. I am a survivor of racism, harassment, discrimination, and sexual violence. My life's work is to help survivors grow wings. From my own healing journey, I recognize intimately the importance of surviving and thriving, resisting shame, coping with distress, and recreating your life. While I value traditional psychotherapy, I also know the healing power of expressive arts, spirituality, community, and culture (Hawkins, 2005). These various points of wisdom, including my personal herstory, lead me to affirm that I need to celebrate that something has tried to kill me and it has failed. It is from this place of both celebration and violation that I come to my identity as both a woman of African descent and a psychologist.

Becoming a Womanist Psychologist

Words formed in our mouths and memories take on various meanings so let me start by saying what I mean when I speak of becoming a womanist psychologist. Becoming is a process that is a lifelong journey. It ebbs and flows, circles back on itself and shoots into the outer spaces of our imagination and aspiration. A womanist is one who has a respect and appreciation for the abilities and strengths of women. A womanist or a feminist of color also adopts an urgent mandate to address sexism, racism, and all forms of marginalization and discrimination, instead of privileging gender issues to the neglect of other forms of oppression. A psychologist from my perspective is a healer who combines the art and science of human transformation. When I identify myself as a womanist psychologist who is in a constant state of becoming, I say this with an awareness that my journey did not begin on the graduate school campus of Duke University.

I was born in Boston and raised primarily in Baltimore, Maryland by two ministers—my father and my mother. I come from a legacy of powerful women, powerful women who recognize the value of using strength to empower others, powerful women who chose to spend their time with powerful men who were not intimidated by their strength. My mother is a womanist theologian—a minister who focuses on understanding the gospel through the lens of liberation for African women. It is the gospel that teaches that Jesus is on the side of the marginalized and not on the side of the oppressor. It is this liberation gospel that declares God's love for African women is not in spite of who we are but because of who we are—beautifully and wonderfully made.

My mother, who grew up one of 10 children in the projects of New York, battled panic attacks and various phobias and yet went on to become an awe-inspiring woman of great accomplishment with over 25 years of dedicated ministry to women. She is an author who has led a global women's organization for decades, started schools on two continents, created self-help initiatives around the globe, and promoted spiritual, educational, and economic empowerment for people of African descent, especially women and girls. Her mother, my grandmother, was also one who battled poverty and discrimination working as a housekeeper in the homes of White families while she watched the demise of her husband, my grandfather who battled PTSD resulting from his service in World War II. My grandmother was a woman of integrity, dignity, character, and leadership. Later in life, she worked for several decades in a residential home for abused and neglected children and also served the community through her dedicated service as a leader in her local Church. My grandmother on my father's side was also a woman who promoted the importance of both family responsibility and empowerment. She was a source of strength to her family and Church and she also was a phenomenal saleswoman for the Shaklee Corporation, selling nutrition products within lower income African American communities where health care was and still is often inadequate. These three women armed me with important principles for life. They taught me to value empowerment, service, community, family, motivation, faith, and action.

I am also a product of the nurturing men in my life. My father and his father were ministers, pastors, and eventually Bishops in the African Methodist Church. They both served as leaders of Churches in both the United States and Africa (West and Southern). They were also both focused on liberation theology, which is based on the belief that the Christian gospel is meant to bring empowerment, freedom, and justice to those who are marginalized. Because of my father and grandfather, I grew up seeing the image of Jesus as an African American man. This is in direct contrast of all of the media images of Black men as incompetent. In my worldview, being a person of African descent came with struggle but also came with strength. It was later during adolescence that I first heard God referred to as "She" by my mother and other womanist theologians. My mother's father used to work as a cook on the railroad but spent the majority of his life and all of my life in a veteran's hospital due to severe PTSD. Even in his silence- and smoke-filled room there was clarity in my grandfather's eyes that only truly made sense to me when my grandmother resurrected his life with her lively descriptions of his dynamic personality and passion before the war. All of these images and words led to my adoption of a critical consciousness that allowed me to see my possibility beyond the narrow parameters that racist and patriarchal structures would try to use to confine me.

As a result of both of my parents being ministers, I grew up being aware of pastoral counseling. People of religious backgrounds and ethnic minorities are often more likely to seek help from religious leaders as opposed to psychologists. Church members and community members often called our home and came to meet with my parents at the Church. If I answered the phone, it was not uncommon to hear someone in distress asking for a listening ear, a prayer, a word of encouragement, or advice. Witnessing and at times being involved in these encounters birthed in me an interest in counseling. Further life experiences, such as multiple encounters with racism, sexual harassment, community violence, and assault, as well as living in Liberia, West Africa at the outbreak of the Civil War, prompted me to focus my study of psychology in the realm of trauma recovery and prevention.

Being a Female Therapist

Often graduate school training in psychology focuses on the worldview of the client and the importance of attachment, rapport, and therapeutic relationship in the healing process. The critical component that is often missing from this discussion is the way clients respond to us as a function of our various identity markers. This oversight in training stems from a view of marginalized communities as "other" and whiteness, maleness, heterosexuality, middle class status, and documented legal status as "norm," unremarkable, and therefore requiring little notice. The assumption that the therapist will be a person of these demographics leads to training that silences the identity of the therapist and focuses exclusively on the pathology of the "other." The truth, which I discovered as I began to practice, is that our multiple identities as therapists greatly shape, influence, and trigger the interactions that occur in therapy. As most of my training in cultural psychology was focused on preparing White therapists to work effectively with ethnic minority clients, none of my supervisors who were all White had spoken to me about what it would be like for me, an African American woman, to work with African American and non–African American clients. I was ill-equipped to handle the White male client who told me he had always been told Black women were sexually "loose" and he wondered if I was "loose." I had not been prepared to deal with the White female client who told me that she was fine working with me because I'm pretty but that the "homely" Black women were the mean ones who seem to have a bad attitude all the time. I had never been given tools to address the Chinese American woman who was dating a Black man and was afraid I would be like "all Black women who hate her for taking their man." Each of these dynamics was based not on my race alone nor my gender alone but the intersection of both of these identity markers. We often hear supervisors and professors speak about the importance of dealing with your issues. This is very true and important advice. It is however incomplete. You have to also deal with the issues that society has attached to your identity. If I had not worked through issues of identity, self-esteem, self-efficacy, and oppression, I would not have been able to have the difficult dialogues that have been a common part of my practice. It takes the phrase "the art and science of therapy" to another level when we consider the task of being healer to someone who fears you and in some cases hates you based on your cultural identity markers. Therapy has to be a safe space to shatter the silence and shame and that includes the silence that exists around stigma, discrimination, and stereotypes.

A great example of this is a counseling encounter I had with a Chinese American young woman who was a survivor of sexual abuse. She told me she had two wishes. She wished her father had never touched her breasts and she wishes she was born White. I had to recognize the trauma of both of these statements and deal with both of them. In talking about the need for her to resist the societal messages that promote a narrow view of beauty as being White, blond, blue eyed, and thin, we had a powerful moment. The client looked up at me said, "Well, Dr. Bryant, do you think you're beautiful?" She couldn't know the full weight of her question. Having come of age as a young woman with dark complexion, natural hair the texture of lamb's wool, and absolutely unmistakable African features, in the inner city of Baltimore, I had battled self-esteem and after much personal struggle had come to see beauty within myself despite the fact that I am opposite of all of the Western notions of beauty. Fortunately I had dealt with these issues years before this therapeutic encounter, so when the client asked her question I could facilitate an informed discussion with her about the difficulty of resisting sexist and racist messages that can chip away at your self-esteem and the very real possibility that one can come to a place of self-validation. This exchange led to an important point in her recovery process and identity formation.

An additional aspect of being a female therapist is the need to balance compassion and boundaries. Women are often socialized to be caretakers, givers, and/or self-sacrificing servants. Many of us who enter the field of counseling have taken these messages to heart. While compassion and giving of yourself to your clients is an important aspect to being a therapist, we have to also be very clear about setting boundaries for the sake of ourselves and our clients. If we are not careful about this, we end up having clients whose sessions run over, who do not pay their bills, and whose inappropriate behavior remains unchallenged. If we are not careful about this we schedule clients during times we were supposed to have lunch breaks or take on the workload of two people while not being adequately compensated for one position. These are professional issues that supervisors have to do a better of job of empowering therapists-in-training to navigate. It is true that women and ethnic minorities are least likely to negotiate for a higher salary when offered a job. As a female therapist, I have to model for myself, my daughter, and my clients what it means to embody some of the traits that are traditionally described as feminine as well as some of those traditionally associated with masculinity. Being an effective therapist for me has meant being both nurturing and challenging, being kind and strong.

Finally being a female therapist for me has meant recognizing the urgency of discussing topics that some therapists consider optional. While trauma happens to males and females, we are all aware that females are more likely to be sexually abused, harassed, and assaulted. We are also more likely to be victims of intimate partner violence, including being more likely to be killed by a current or former intimate partner. My awareness of this as well as my life journey as a survivor motivates me to support and engage in routine screening. I continue to be frustrated by the web of silence that leads many therapists to not ask about trauma history while using the blanket excuse that it is not the presenting problem. This excuse puts the responsibility of disclosure in the hands of the survivor even though research and clinical experience continues to demonstrate the emotional, social, and physiological barriers survivors face in their attempts to discuss traumatic memories. As a female therapist, a survivor, and one who strives to engage in ethical care, I take the responsibility of letting clients know that therapy is a safe place to discuss those areas of our lives that have so often been silenced. The way I begin to break the silence is by asking the questions. Judith Herman, author of *Trauma and Recovery*, reminded us that it is easy to side with the perpetrator. All they ask us for is our silence. As a therapist, I have to take ownership for the power of the questions I choose to ask as well as the issues I choose to silence.

The Female Healing Experience

As a psychologist, a person of faith, a womanist, and a survivor, I approach the therapeutic process from the perspective of one who believes in resurrection. I am aware of the realities of trauma, stress, and oppression but I consider myself a realist with wings. There are so many ugly violations that assault our spirits, minds, hearts, and bodies and yet I can sing like Louis Armstrong, "and I think to myself what a wonderful world." As therapists I believe we have to represent the hope in the room. People come looking for possibility. They want to know can life be more than it is right now. We receive so many messages of doom. I see the role of a therapist as being a truth teller, healing presence, and a guide out of the difficult shadows. I seek to both be very present in the midnight of people's experiences and to remind them that midnight is the start of a new morning. This is one thing that therapists and religious persons have in common—the belief in miracles and transformation. The issue just becomes which pathway we take to get to the healing. I refuse to believe we have to live as victims, as walking wounded. I believe we are living miracles. Given our life circumstances, statistics predict our demise, but the healers among us remind us of our possibility. I strive to be an encourager, a way maker, a healing balm, a space for truth, a motivator, and skills builder, equipping people to live with holistic health, which means living well in all areas of our lives.

To do this requires that I invite people to come into the space, physically and psychically with their whole selves. No part of us can be left behind if we are to be whole. I know professionally and personally the cost of secret shame, the cost of disconnection, and the cost of both self-sabotage and oppression. As a result, I know that for real change to be present we have to be fully present, reconciling past valleys, present realities, and future hopes. The truth is we are complex beings with competing, sometimes contradictory beliefs, values, feelings, and behaviors. Effective care and ethical care requires creating safe space where the complexity of our humanity can be present as we move toward healing and recovery.

As therapists each of us comes to the encounter with particular gifts. The key is to marry our identity and gifts with the art and science of healing work. One of the gifts I bring to the table is a genuine compassion for people. Our personality comes through our work directly or indirectly. I am saddened when I hear therapists speaking who clearly don't like dealing with people. People are discerning and can tell when we are not invested from a place of the heart. As Cornel West (2010) says, "You can't lead the people if you don't love the people." I can teach people some skills from a detached place but I cannot motivate them to see the necessity of the skills or to believe that they can successfully use them, if I don't come to the interaction from a place of genuine care.

Another gift I bring to the table is the firsthand knowledge that recovery is possible. When therapists are just starting off they have read about counseling theories and strategies but they don't know firsthand that these principles will work unless they have lived it. As a result of being a survivor and having been blessed to work with so many on their healing journeys, I bring to the counseling process an understanding that while it is a process, healing, recovery, and transformation can take place. We are not who we were before our difficulties, traumas, disappointments, but we can take those experiences and shape a new approach to our lives that some call post-traumatic growth.

An additional gift I bring to the table is a respect for alternative healing strategies. In my healing journey from sexual assault, things like spirituality, social support, community engagement, and the expressive arts were all critical in addition to traditional psychotherapy. From a reflection on human history as well as the contemporary realities of most people on the planet, I know that many people have lived through great difficulty without the assistance of therapy. This is not said to discount the role of therapists but to instill in us a respect for the various ways people have survived, coped, and even thrived. When we don't have a respect for these pathways, we make the mistaken assumption that those who have not been in therapy before have not done any work on their issues. Instead it is important to build on the cultural and personal strengths that people bring to the table so that we add to their healing repertoire instead of trying to supplant the one they have already built. It is important for people to recognize that they don't have to give up everything they know but instead they can be empowered to choose between the things they want to release, the things they want to modify, the things they want to keep, and the new things they want to gain. Fundamentally this means I know there is more than one way to live a healthy life and this allows me to have true respect for my clients and their journeys.

Theoretical, Conceptual and Practical Applications

As a psychologist, I had to find my voice, my pace, and my personality in the room. My therapeutic framework is based on an ecological model and further a feminist therapy model. In terms of my theoretical orientation, I identify myself as integrative or eclectic, combining psychodynamic and cognitive-behavioral approaches. The therapeutic tools I use include the expressive arts and strengths-based affirmation.

I mentioned in the beginning of this chapter that I am a woman of African descent. I affirm this not merely as a part of my genetic ancestry but also a part of my chosen values. Africentrism, much like many Native American or indigenous traditions, promotes a belief in the connection of all things (Cokley, 2005). We are not separate entities but instead we are all partners in creating ourselves, each other, and the world we live in. We are co-constructing reality and participating in reciprocal socialization. As a result of this awareness, I have to adopt an ecological framework in my work with clients. To share from a personal perspective I know that I am in part the manifestation of my thoughts and choices but additionally I recognize that I am in part a manifestation of my parents' dreams, my grandparents' nightmares, the edification and miseducation provided by my schooling, the expectations taught by my faith tradition, the political realities shaped by Carter, Reagan, Bush, Clinton, Bush, and Obama, the intersecting class realities of a mother who grew up in poverty and a father who grew up middle-class, as well as my encounters with the spirit who is higher than I—the one I call at times Jehovah Shalom which means God my peace.

One of the courses I have taught is Cross Cultural Psychology. One of the things I teach in this class is that there are three layers to our identity. We are all human beings, we are all members of multiple cultural groups, and we are all unique individual beings. When I recognize this, I realize the need for an ecological framework to recognize the way the person, family, couple, or group with whom I am working has been shaped and is simultaneously shaping the world around them.

Connected to this ecological framework, I have also adopted a framework based on feminist psychology (Meyer & Post, 2006). Feminist therapy requires that I both bring to my awareness and bring to my client's awareness the impact of roles, scripts, stereotypes, discrimination, privilege, and oppression. Some would dismiss this as excuse making or political agendas, but as therapists we are supposed to deal with the truth. It is untruthful to see a woman battling body image issues and pretend that it's all in her head while ignoring all of the social messages and realities that have created and supported her thinking. From a feminist psychology perspective, I approach counseling with an awareness of oppression and a simultaneous respect and celebration of the gifts, intelligence, and possibility of those who are often systematically devalued. There would not be such a mass attempt to silence us, if we were not powerful, gifted, valuable, worthy. In essence, healing requires that I acknowledge the wounds and at the same time not reduce the client to the total of their wounds. The struggles we face affect us but do not define us.

In terms of my theoretical orientation, I subscribe to an integrative approach which means I resist Western notions of either/or thinking that is based in false dichotomies and distorted choices. When we are not careful we can find ourselves participating in academic gang wars and clinical social clubs' initiations that require those in training and those in practice to make distinctions and choices that in reality are not mutually exclusive. Africentrism frames things for me on a continuum (Neblett, Hammond, Seaton, & Townsend, 2010). For example, secularity and spirituality are not opposites in Africentrism in the way that they are often presented in Eurocentric circles. Likewise, I find it meaningless to make someone choose between psycho-education and life skills and healing the wounds and conflict of the past that continue to manifest in their present. I take a holistic approach to healing and as a result I recognize and utilize the importance of both a psycho-dynamic orientation and a cognitive-behavioral orientation. I had the pleasure of being taught and supervised by persons who were experts in both orientations and instead of being caught up in the illusion that one path will be the right path for every client without benefit from any other approach, I choose to integrate the two. The level of integration or the domination of one over another varies based on the client, their personality, and treatment goals. From my personal experience, recovery from sexual assault included getting to the unacknowledged shame that I was carrying from multiple experiences, as well as challenging my distorted cognitions and learning new behaviors to replace the maladaptive ones. Ideally I prefer an integrative approach but for those who do not subscribe to such an approach I think it is just important that we have mutual respect for each other's ways of working. Hearing therapists put down therapists of different theoretical orientations gives me the same negative feeling I have when I hear people of one religious tradition putting down people of other faiths. From my personal journey, my Africentric values, and my clinical experience, I see the value of integrating orientations with the aim of treating the whole person—mind, emotion, behavior, id, ego, and superego. I find it critical to attend to cognitive-behavioral solutions, empowerment, thinking, and skills development. I also know as a woman of African descent that marginalized groups often develop what W.E.B. Du Bois called a double consciousness, a need to navigate two worlds based on both what you know of yourself and how the dominant society sees you (Du Bois, 1996). This is demonstrated with the words of poet Paul Laurence Dunbar who wrote: "We wear the mask that grins and lies, that hides our teeth and shades our eyes. . . . With torn and bleeding hearts we smile. . . . " (Dunbar, 1913, p. 71). Given the balancing act of internal and external conflicts that all people and especially stigmatized people have to face, it is also essential to work through the powerful and pervasive issues occurring under the surface.

Two additional aspects of my practice is the use of both a strengths-based approach and expressive arts techniques. As a womanist, I know that women, ethnically marginalized persons, and many others have experienced violation, have been denied, disrespected, and devalued. For therapy to be a therapeutic, it is necessary for me to start from a place of recognizing the strength of my client and empowering them to see their strengths as well (Jones, Hardiman, & Carpenter, 2007). People in general, and trauma survivors in particular, often engage in self-blame and debilitating guilt trips. We judge ourselves on unachievable measures and then walk in shame that robs us from seeing ourselves for who we really are. A part of healing is coming to peace with the ways we have survived and honoring the parts of us that have enabled us to survive and in some cases thrive. It takes a lot for people to work past the fear and stigma associated with seeking counseling and come for their first session. To engage clients in the process it is so important for clients to know that we see their strength.

I also utilize the expressive arts in the therapeutic process and teach graduate students how to make use of the expressive arts (Bryant-Davis,

2005). I am a poet, dancer, and actress who also enjoys music and the visual arts. As a rape survivor, I think one of the reasons I never came to a place of hating my body is because I was a dancer. My body allowed me to give language to the things I had experienced even when I did not have the words to express my experience. Although I was frozen in the moment of violation, as a dancer I also knew my body to be a place of strength and value. Additionally, poetry provided a safe outlet for me to tell my story in metaphors and symbols that could be as revealing or concealing as I wanted. The arts provide a vehicle to speak the unspoken and to express emotions that are often denied in our routine lives. With my clients, both adults and children, artists and those who don't feel artistically inclined at all, I offer the expressive arts as a way to enhance affect awareness, regulation, and communication. I used to keep my identity as an artist and psychologist very segregated. It was a wonderful homecoming for me when I gave myself permission to let my artistic and psychological identities inform and strengthen each other. I strive to help clients also move from divided realities to integrated, whole conceptions of themselves.

Moments of Wisdom and Intimacy: A Few Words for Female Healers

I would like to offer a few closing words to women who are considering entering the field of psychotherapy and those who are currently in graduate school or on internship. The first thing I would like to offer for those who are thinking of entering the field is to remember that your education is an integral component to your professional development. There is a growing popularity for people to become coaches and consultants, which are professions that do not require specific education or training. I would encourage you whether your aim is to be a therapist, psychologist, social worker, coach, or consultant, to recognize the value of training and preparation. In economic times we can sometimes look for shortcuts, but know that what you put in is often what you will get out. To give your clients ethical and competent care it is important that you seek out educational preparation and supervision.

Another important point is to not lose you in the training process. You will have many professors and supervisors. They have wisdom from experience and training so you want to be open to learning from what they have to offer. On the other hand, you don't want to feel like an imposter in the therapy room who is just imitating your supervisors. You want to integrate what you learn and still discover the art of being yourself in the room. Who you are as a therapist should not be totally contrary to who you are as a person. People respond to authenticity so you want to hold firmly to the theories and applications you learn while letting them come alive in the unique person that is you. I once had a colleague who shared a hallway with me share that she was shocked to hear laughter coming from my office given my primary work is with trauma survivors. There is no rule that therapy has to always be this heavy place of doom and gloom to get work done. Some of the most therapeutic moments can come in seasons of silence and seasons of heartfelt laughter. We are to model for our clients what it means to be healthy human beings; this means we have a range of emotions and are not robots or blank slates in the room writing on notepads with emptiness in our eyes. Strive to be always present, full alive and in the moment. Thinking of the next brilliant thing to say will make you miss what the client just said. Show up and let your clients know that you are connected to them on a heart level first and then from there we build on the other components.

The final thought I would like to share with my sister healers who are already working in the field is often worded as "self-care." We hear this phrase but I want to encourage you to internalize it (Carroll, Gilroy, & Murra, 1999). *You are worthy of care.* You deserve breath, music, laughter, silence, a listening ear, movement, and healing waters. You need to press pause before you burn out. You do not need to be everything to everyone. You cannot and should not be therapist to everyone you encounter including co-workers, mates, extended family, friends, and friends of friends. It's too much. You cannot give what you do not receive. Be intentional about taking time and space to restore and feed your soul. Also be intentional about setting boundaries and saying "no" to some things so you can be free to say "yes" to the things that really nurture your spirit. I have personally learned the necessity of self-care and I want to share with you the strategies that work for me:

Starting the day with morning spiritual devotions such as reading and prayer
Using the arts to express the feelings and thoughts I am carrying as a result of the work
Taking time off for fun and relaxation
Building and maintaining supportive relationships that are reciprocal instead of those in which I am the caretaker
Engaging in prevention and advocacy work to combat despair and gain empowerment

I encourage you to try these strategies and/or develop strategies that work for you. The key is to be disciplined enough to maintain them over time. Being busy is not the time to cut out self-care. On the contrary, being busy is a call to be even more vigilant about taking care of yourself.

We are blessed to be able to do this healing work. It is a gift that people allow us to bear witness and accompany them on their journey. I am glad every day for the vocational choice I made to be a healer. In truth, I believe it is a calling and a legacy. I come from a chain of those who whispered empowerment in my ears and braided revolution in my braids. I am a woman, an African woman living in America and daily I am simultaneously healed, healing, and healer.

References

Bryant-Davis, T. (2005). *Thriving in the wake of trauma: A multicultural guide.* Westport, CT: Praeger Publishers/Greenwood Publishing Group.

Carroll, L., Gilroy, P., & Murra, J. (1999). The moral imperative: Self-care for women psychotherapists. *Women & Therapy, 22*(2), 133–143.

Cokley, K. (2005). Racial(ized) identity, ethnic identity, and Afrocentric values: Conceptual and methodological challenges in understanding African American identity. *Journal of Counseling Psychology, 52*(4), 517–526.

Du Bois, W. E. B. (1996). *The souls of Black folk.* New York: Penguin Books.

Dunbar, P. L. (1913). We Wear the Mask. In *The complete poems of Paul Laurence Dunbar* (p. 71). New York: Dodd, Mead and Co. Also available (Retrieved on 4/6/10) from http://www.potw.org/archive/potw8.html.

Hawkins, S. (2005). Uncovering the journey: The experience of women of African descent who have participated in alternative healing. *Dissertation Abstracts International,* 66.

Jones, L., Hardiman, E., & Carpenter, J. (2007). Mental health recovery: A strengths-based approach to culturally relevant services for African Americans. *Journal of Human Behavior in the Social Environment, 15*(2–3), 251–269.

Meyer, E., & Post, L. (2006). Alone at night: A feminist ecological model of community violence. *Feminist Criminology, 1*(3), 207–227.

Neblett, E., Hammond, W., Seaton, E., & Townsend, T. (2010). Underlying mechanisms in the relationship between Africentric worldview and depressive symptoms. *Journal of Counseling Psychology, 57*(1), 105–113.

West, Cornel (2010). Quotable Quote. Retrieved on 4/6/10 from http://www.goodreads.com/quotes/show/49495.

Hannah Krants' Conversion

2

JANICE CRAWFORD

For me the path of becoming and developing as a psychotherapist has been a case of soul Braille: feeling my way along until I can open my eyes underwater. And as I distinguish each at first mysterious form, I find that one way of looking at life is to look at life's multiple levels. Like the currents of the oceans, some movements are more affected by surface phenomena, while others are like currents that run deep, slow and silent. Beyond our ordinary imagination, these currents hardly seem influenced by what occurs where the waves meet the horizon. And in a simplification, we might call the surface current the level of entanglements and the later the level of the life force itself.

The entanglement level reflects the human drama. Here our sense of belonging is based on blind loyalties that feed off exclusion. The effects of traumas, blame and justification, perpetration and victimization, reactivity, and concretized inner images—particularly of our parents and lineages—prevail. Attempts to gain or maintain power, tragic misunderstandings and confusion dominate not only individuals but the groups to which we are consciously or unconsciously trying to belong or maintain our belonging. At its worst on this level, we are involved in violent actions toward each other and the earth, each of us some ever-shifting landscape of brutality and beauty.

And though these currents are interpenetrating, the current of the life force has different qualities. This is the force Christians call "the mind of God" or "grace" and Buddhists call "true nature." And some might call this level universal intelligence or pure energy. Our fullest selves, we are supported by those who came before us in a timeless love. Whether conscious of attunement to it or not, to the degree we honor this reality we are drawn by something toward something. Expansion is the nature of this level, and we are unique movements in that expansion. We are particular yet inseparable from all else and in the right place with those who came before us and those who have or will come after us. Additionally, it may be that the sensitivity that women therapists can often bring to human relationships is a great asset in working with these sometimes subtle to discriminate currents.

And it's important to say as we begin that at 67 I'm consistently happy and often thrilled by my life and work. I've never loved my work more or felt more in my right place as a woman and as a therapist. And I know what my true role as a therapist is and what I am contributing to life. I've pursued many areas of study and a number of careers. And I've had many brilliant and generous teachers in both psychology and matters more definitively of the soul. Other teachers have been my therapists, partners, and clients. And four years ago in a casual afternoon get-together with a friend and colleague, Cristina Casanova, my capacity to understand and to love quietly exploded as she placed a small plastic figure on the table to represent my father. In giving me a glimpse of Bert Hellinger's work she placed a similar figure representing my father's father—a Missouri constable who was ambushed in 1916 when my father was two—about two inches behind him and facing his back. And as I observed these figures in this relation to each other I began to experience a sea change.

I began to quietly weep as the visual reality of the two figures touched a place no words or therapeutic concepts had ever reached: I could *see* how lost the father that I had mightily struggled with for the first 40 years of my life had been, how much he longed for his never-mentioned father. Admittedly more mysteriously, I could also *feel* the repair of love occurring in what I would later be able to understand as my first conscious experience of the "field" surrounding those two representative figures.

Soon thereafter I began to study with Hellinger facilitator, Suzi Tucker, in her Learning Circle. One moving constellation after the other with human representatives began immediately to reveal truths far beyond my consciousness and internal images at that time. I began to have a sense of my prodigal journey and what I was blindly carrying on that journey. And my lens as a therapist began to expand from its focus on the individual to include the multi-generational trauma and from the pathology to the strength and love in every family.

As I began to slowly discriminate between the entanglement level and what was occurring on the life force level I saw that on that latter level, despite 40 years of intensive therapy and spiritual work, in relation to my father, mother, and lineages I had moved very little. It would be only recently, for example, that I would come to understand the full impact on my mother—and on me—of the secret she carried. And I would begin to see her diagnosis—and the diagnostic system in general—of "clinical depression and anxiety" when I was 10 in a very different light.

In terms of my relationship with my mother, with the exception of one exquisite moment and a blessed year of greater closeness in 2002 before she died at 84, from as early as I can remember I kept a deadening distance from my mother and what I experienced as her devouring needs. Despite her immense sacrifice and kindness, I early became a distant relative within my own family. Though as an adult I had become dutiful and polite in a lifeless obligatory way until her last year, we both knew how much I kept my heart protected from her even then. Only recently would I understand that the greater part of that protection was my utter helplessness in the face of a need no one "in front of" her could ever fill.

It would take four years of Bert Hellinger's work and Carmen, a Catalan woman with whom I did not even share a common language, to repair the tragically interrupted reaching out movement toward my mother and to begin to truly join my mother in what Suzi calls "the great reciprocity of love." And far beyond that, because of Carmen's sensitive representation of my mother at Hellinger's Intensive Training in Barcelona in 2009, I would begin to know who and what my mother and all mothers really are.

A German classically trained psychoanalyst who is now more recognized as a phenomenological philosopher, writer, and teacher, Bert Hellinger has pioneered work that is spreading throughout the world. At 85 he conducts dozens of trainings, from Sri Lanka to Mongolia. Last year, for example, in Argentina over one thousand people gave him a 15-minute standing ovation before he could begin. He has written over 50 books that are translated into, at last count, 22 languages, including Arabic and Chinese. And there are now many books about him and by others expanding his insights into every imaginable area, from peacekeeping to spiritual transcendence.

Hellinger studied many therapeutic approaches during and after he left 16 years as a Catholic priest with the Zulu. His work in family systems was influenced by Thea Schonfelder, Ruth McKlendon, Les Kadis, Jakob Moreno, Eric Berne, Virginia Satir, Ivan Boszormeni-Nagy, and others. And from early in his career his phenomenological work focused on the subject of personal and group conscience. These inquiries took him into the domain of understanding the deeper forces at work beneath the levels with which much of the groundbreaking earlier family constellation work was engaged. During these observations, most of which are beyond the scope of this chapter, he began to observe what he calls Orders of Love. The recurring pattern he observed was that three things constitute a prerequisite for the flow of love on the level I have called the life force level: belonging, balance, and order.

He also observed that people with no prerequisite knowledge or skills could step into the constellation circle as a representative of a family member, quality, organization, event, or even country and be moved by a knowing force, the deeper currents of which I spoke, in directions that helped heal generations-old injuries to what he calls the family soul. His insights about this field of knowledge are consistent with biologist Rupert Sheldrake's morphogenic field research (1981), systems theorist Ervin Laszlo's (2009) "Akashic experience" observations, Franz Ruppert's (2008) writings on the possible quantum physics explanation of the field, among others.

Hellinger (2008) describes what occurs for representatives in the field of what he now calls spiritual family constellations as follows:

> They are allowed their time, and all of a sudden, they may be drawn by a movement, as if it came from outside, without their being able to direct this movement or resist it. . . . In this way, they experience being in tune with an outside force that initiates a movement through them. But this only happens if they remain collected, without intentions of their own and without fear of what might show up. As soon as intentions come into play, for example, the intention to help, or to attempt to control what might come to light, the connection with the movements of the spirit is lost. (pp. 62–63)

Because of the breadth of his work—and of the creative expansions of this work by many others—it is difficult in a brief chapter to give the reader anything but a hint of this cosmology. These however are a few of the questions the study of his work began to raise for me as a therapist:

Is my empathy focused on the historic system rather than exclusively on the client?

Am I aware that at some point my understanding and empathy may keep my client attached to their entangled narratives?

Am I remembering that everyone feels 50% loyalty to each parent underneath their unconscious loyalties and needs to have full access to both parents' lineages?

Do I remember that ultimately any unconscious feeling of superiority over their parents or lineage interferes with the client experiencing true support and fullness?

Does my work help connect my client to their system or collude with disconnection?

Do I always give my client's parents and ancestors—especially the excluded ones—a place of respect in my heart, regardless of what is said about them?

Do I consistently remember that my client and I are ultimately guided by forces much greater then either of us?

Earlier Careers and the Women's Movement

I propelled myself as soon as I could from my hometown, a small California oil town, to San Francisco. And over the years to come I would feel my way through—or some might say, be moved through, a number of diverse and satisfying careers, each contributing something important to my work now. At 18 in San Francisco I began as a secretary and worked my way up to being a licensed real estate manager. This work ended, however, after an experience of what we could later call sexual discrimination and harassment. In the wake of that anger and disappointment I moved to London, worked there for a year, and then moved to New York City in the mid-1960s.

In New York I again worked up the ladder as far as I could, ultimately becoming a senior associate media director in advertising with an office on Madison Avenue. As well as enjoying the work and play, years later I would also be grateful that this experience in what has come to be known as the "Mad Men" era helped me understand the experiences of my clients in the business world. However, I had hit the glass ceiling—women were not considered for jobs in broadcast sales, the logical next step for me at that time. Intending it to be a minimal gesture, I told the New York City National Organization for Women I would do a bit to help with their Media Committee.

Within a few months I was deeply involved in everything from radio and television appearances to coalition organizing. My experience as a media buyer helped me teach women how to get millions of dollars of television and radio play locally for NOW's public service media campaign for women's equality. And as a Member of the Board of NOW New York City, I formed a group of 14 women-identified groups and testified against broadcasters' hiring practices and the image of women in the media at the House of Representatives in Washington, D.C. Broadcasters were my clients, and unsurprisingly I was fired not long afterward. I went from Madison Avenue to creating a feminist lemonade stand in Greenwich

Village and to several years of organizing and theorizing. During this time I was also interviewed about the earlier harassment experience in San Francisco by the *Wall Street Journal* and by Jane Pauley on the *Today Show*, appearing with a friend, Lin Farley, who brought the issue to national attention with her book *The Sexual Shakedown*. Some of my other work in the movement is described in *Feminists Who Changed America* (Love, 2006).

It was sometimes harrowing, but being among brilliant minds like Kate Millett, Phyllis Chesler, Mary Daly, Ty Grace Atkinson, Charlotte Bunch, and so many others was thrilling beyond description. Creativity and courage were tested over and over, and with these passionate, fun, inspiring women I learned that with others I can change consensual reality—sometimes quickly and sometimes slowly. The experience of the women's movement helped me know my clients can do that as well. On some level, however, I piously felt that I was self-made, the first person—let alone woman—in my family to risk everything for what she believed. It would be almost 40 years before I understood how foolish this idea was or before I cared or knew about my great-great-grandmothers Hannah and Mary and so many others—including my parents—so much braver than I.

And while knowledge about one's family or even parentage is not necessary to do the Hellinger work, I was fortunate to have one lineage of Mormon relatives for whom the Mormons had especially meticulous records. In the research I would come to relish, I found, for example, that Hannah, who was born in Germany, converted to Mormonism in the 1860s. This was a dangerous act in many countries at that time. Selling their estate to escape persecution, she and her husband were able to help six other families similarly at risk immigrate with them to America. Their five-year-old son, Christian, died and was buried at sea—an experience records indicate his sister, my great-grandmother "Tear," never forgot. There were fires and starvation aboard ship, deaths as they walked across America—sometimes barefoot—and ultimately an extermination order put out against Mormons by the Governor of Missouri. Yet they persevered and life went on.

Becoming a Therapist

To support myself while completing my B.A. and M.S.W., I became a licensed medical massage therapist. I loved the work: one particularly sweet pleasure was working with Anne Bancroft between acts of *Golda*. And this work taught me sensitivity to the inherent intelligence of the body. It would also prove to be of enormous help in identifying subtle fight, flight, or freeze impulses in the somatic trauma work I would do years later.

And it was during this period that I decided to become a therapist. While there were some entanglement level reasons for this decision, on the life force level it is clear to me now that I was just following the natural flow of guidance. For example, something made me know I needed to become more intimate with death, and so I requested my second social work internship at Memorial Sloan-Kettering Cancer Center and found myself smack in the middle of the beginning of the AIDS epidemic. In the early months we didn't know how AIDS was being transmitted and whether we were being exposed when we entered the room of a patient with AIDS. And there was the closeness of being on the front lines with many remarkable staff and patients. Being able to study with Elisabeth Kubler-Ross and being given the opportunity to start the first HIV-positive group on the East Coast were blessings for which I will always feel grateful.

However, despite the many satisfactions in my life and work, in those years I was also struggling with a pull towards what my therapists and I labeled "depression." They would listen and be empathic to my helplessness and outrage about my father's cruelty and my mother's need "to use my soul as a life raft." We had no way of knowing then that this narrative would at some point become the problem rather than the solution. Stuck in a one-dimensional view on the entanglement level, those fixed inner images of my parents did not allow me to see them fully and therefore access and honor their strength and love. Hellinger (2008) writes, "As soon as people are cut off from one or both their parents they lose energy and strength. They are weak and develop symptoms" (p. 156). I know also now that I was blindly saying to my mother, "I'll do it like you. Out of love I will carry this longing and shame for you and your mother and her mother. . . ."

In addition, paradoxically, on some level I was unconsciously using psychological understanding to avoid seeing something more fundamental—I was seeking a kind of psychological bypass. And because of this, however successful I was, I believed I was scrambling "on my own" in the world, unconsciously fighting what I feared would be involved in any sense of true tethering to anything greater than the self I was attempting to create. Fortunately I also had a resilience I now know to be the true legacy from my family—as each of us does or we would not be here.

Like my ancestors I kept searching, enjoying a great deal within these movements of discovery. For example, study in a small group with Jessica Benjamin, the author of *Bonds of Love* (1988), was theoretically compelling and a great personal pleasure. And my own psychoanalytic study at the Training and Research Institute for Self Psychology (TRISP) was among the most creative periods of my early career. I later taught Gender Studies at T.R.I.S.P. in a deeply rewarding collaboration with analyst and writer Doris Brothers.

While there, I wrote a radical and complex gender theory that I presented at the 1995 Chicago National Self Psychology Conference. The paper was later published as, "The Severed Self: Gender as Trauma" (Crawford, 1996). I proposed three levels of "gender fantasy": the performance, selfobject, and restorative dimensions. Referencing Heinz Kohut's proposed grandiose and deflated aspects of self in the "vertical split," I equated contemporary masculinity with an untransformed grandiose fantasy of self and femininity with an untransformed deflated fantasy of self. And though I believe there were some provocative explorations of identity and identification on the entanglement level in this paper, my—I now know to be historical—hurt and anger at the time I wrote this chapter created an ungenerous theoretical perspective on what I now understand to be the possible *default* positions for many men and women.

Gratefully because of Hellinger's work I am now able to enjoy leaning my head on the shoulder of the representative for my father and safely relax into what was always there on the life force level. I can more fully understand men's suffering, especially when they cannot protect life, and appreciate their contributions to my life and to all life. And I can now honor my mother and every woman—including myself—as the creative crucible of life, whether or not we give birth. Mothers risk their lives to bring life forth and sustain life—often under horrific conditions—and those of us who do not give birth support life in a multitude of other ways.

Returning to my analytic training, I now feel that to some extent I unconsciously used self-psychology transference theory to justify taking a re-parenting stance with my clients: I could be the better parent—more empathic and a better mirror. I think I particularly enjoyed the being idealized phase of my clients working through their (in Kohutian terms) natural narcissism. And I didn't have to risk my life to give birth, diaper, or put my clients through college. And, unlike most mothers, I was paid rather well for my efforts.

There would be a major shift in the orientation of my work, however, in the late 1990s. Impressed by the effectiveness of traumatologist Peter Levine's (1997) work, Somatic Experiencing (SE), I became one of the first two licensed psychotherapists at that time certified to do his work in New York City. I'm very pleased that during the next few years I was able to contribute to the building of a community of SE trained trauma therapists in this area that now numbers in the hundreds.

From Levine's work I came to understand something about the danger of being human: we all bear unrepaired experiences of overwhelm in our nervous systems, be they chronically difficult emotional environments or acute shocks. These traumas are frozen in the body and manifest in a multitude of symptoms. I learned that psychotherapy will not be effective long-term if it doesn't include work with the body and its natural ability to release fight, flight, and freeze instincts that could not be fully completed at the time (Crawford, 2005). I would come to see more recently that traumas in the historic family also create fragmentations or freezes in the life force that passed along through the generations. In a similar way that the life force in the body knows how to heal itself, the life force in the family soul knows how to heal its blockages.

Many Paths

Immersed for over 40 years in very rich and deeply satisfying spiritual teachings primarily in the Buddhist or Advaita Vedanta traditions (see Crawford, 2005), I was until recently a student for 14 years in the school of A. H. Almaas. Also a phenomenological philosopher, his method is called the Diamond Approach. This work represents his integration of teachings from the world's spiritual traditions, an extensive knowledge of depth psychology and thousands of hours of work of personal inquiry into unfolding dimensions of reality. A student of master teacher Alia Johnson, it is impossible to describe the impact of this work on my life. I can say that it did help me become more physically present in my body in this reality. Guiding me into glimpses of unquestioned inseparability, it helped me begin to discriminate some of the levels of experience I described earlier. And many friendships in this journey nourished and supported me in incalculable ways. From my beloved friend and ex-Benedictine nun Ruth Wilson, for example, I received the most intelligent kindness one could ever imagine. And with philosopher and Zen Sensei Nancy Baker I shared a love of truth and a world of inspiration.

Like aspects of my personal therapy, however, I now see that one element, the spiritual work, also involved the unconscious hope I could reach clarity and peace by going around or above (i.e., transcending) my family, my mother in particular. I have described this attempted detour in the poem about my mother on the following page as "looking into many faces and many faiths."

One of 13 children, my mother lost her mother at 11. Very poor, she was forced to leave school in seventh grade and was shuffled from sister to sister. Though I would not know this secret until my fifties, what made this even more desperate was that her father had tried to attack her as a child. He was in and out of jail for child molestation, eventually being imprisoned in San Quentin. I would learn after my mother's death that when he was released in 1949 it is rumored he was killed by police, paying the full price for his actions. Out of love and a shame that did not belong to her, my mother carried to her grave the secret of her father's crimes from her husband and everyone but me.

What I have appreciated only recently is that, despite this great suffering, my mother's capacity for love endured. She sustained a lifelong marriage. She gave birth to and reared three children who, in turn, contribute to life. She stayed despite her natural desire to be with her mother. She didn't stop loving me. And, though my movement toward my mother was interrupted very early in my life, this recent poem describes the result of my step-by-step movements back to her in numerous constellations that led up to the constellation with Carmen. In that constellation I was finally able to look past the pain and disappointment in her eyes that had always terrified and overwhelmed me. I was able to see the boundless depth of her love and wisdom:

Until This Moment
did not trust your eyes
The eyes I then looked for
In many faces and many faiths
I did not know
You would wait forever
That a mother always holds
Everything her child feels
Carrying her own life
The vastness
The shattered and indestructible
The context
Not like god
god
And I though childless
Now in greater fullness
Wider into woman
A more enfolding eye
(Originally published in The Knowing Field: International Constellations Journal, *January, 2010, London. Reprinted with permission)*

Hellinger (2009) has proposed, "Those who have reservations about their mothers, also have reservations about life and happiness. Just as their mothers withdraw from them as a result of their reservations and rejection, so life and success withdraw from them as well" (p.12). And as I now enjoy the homecoming of feeling my cheek resting against hers at last, I understand fully the meaning of these words.

These experiences have also led me to question a developmental theory that demands absolute separation from the mother as the sine qua non of maturity and the only non-pathological option. A more comprehensive description of healthy development may be that our mothers as they are—whether dead or live and neither idealized or demonized—are the energetic through line for us to the life force. As the interrupted movement toward them is completed in conscious slow embodied steps, we not only move toward them but into and beyond them into the widest landscape. Here absolute separation from anyone—including mother—defies the ultimate reality of the inseparable field where we are one soul.

Therefore, perhaps a more experience-near theory of development would include 1) Particularization, 2) Extension into the world, and 3) Expansion that includes the continuous inclusion that moves beyond the possible blind loyalties of the family, group, or nation. All these phases are lifelong and include a grateful integration of all that came before and an increasingly refined alignment with the greater forces. And it may be that women therapists in general might have socialized and innate qualities that can support this more comprehensive sense of development. Because our role has been more maintaining the continuity of life and relationships than protecting life, women who stand in our female lineages may be able to be more responsive to some of the subtle nuances of the long view and forward movement of life. We may be allowed to grieve more easily—one of the prerequisites for allowing true movement on other levels. And as women we have the advantage of a lesser demand for separation from mother than men.

In regard to men's roles, Tucker (personal communication) has suggested that her work in facilitating thousands of constellations has indicated, "Men feel their role as protector as being central, and any movement away from that is a movement away from the ease of organic permission from men who came before. The permission is there, but it may have to be revealed. . . . Women are the means and children are the manifestation: men are most essential in their immediate stewardship."

Two Case Vignettes

An accomplished Jewish intellectual in his late eighties in ill health, a great deal stood in the way of Harold feeling connected to his parents and history. He was fortunate that the woman representing his mother felt in contact with his mother's great love for him. At first reverting to an old strategy of staying in his mind, I put my hand on his head, bowing it slightly, and asked him to become quiet and just silently look in her eyes. As he did this it slowly became hard for him to deny the love emanating from her. He was able to see this for the first time and respond in a very deep way. Clearly astonished, at the end of the evening he said, "Before all I could see behind me was tragedy. Now I see love."

Ellen, an ethereally beautiful young woman in her early twenties, came into treatment because her mother, Ann, had recently committed suicide. Ellen sensed very early that her mother was "going to leave": she spoke of smelling her mother's sweater when she was just seven years old, feeling she would one day need to remember that scent.

Using Somatic Experiencing (SE) to find ways to work with releasing the terrible shock and overwhelm in her body helped her begin to know that she could deal with the intensity of feelings she was having and begin to find the literal ground beneath her again—no matter how acutely disoriented she felt and no matter how much at moments she might want to follow her mother when the longing or pain became too great.

Because Ann's mother had died shortly after Ann was born, there would have been a huge force drawing toward her mother. So in addition to working with Ellen in the roller coaster of feelings and using SE with the primal instincts arising, we are also able to acknowledge that on the life force level it was heroic of Ann to stay long enough to accompany her children into their young adulthood, giving them enough. Ellen appreciates that we can see this together in the broader landscape of her love for her mother. Movements in constellations are showing Ellen she does not have to follow her mother to love her and have her with her always and gradually we see a diminishing fragility and her increasing commitment to presence in this world. So what has become clearer to me in these last few years is the following:

My job is to help people with broken connections to their bodies, families, and sense of meaning. While I can sometimes be temporarily helpful, I am not the mother. My right-sized and right-placed relationship to my mother, father, and lineage are my greatest resources as a person and as a therapist. Without this I will be restricted to the entanglement level with my clients. Suzi Tucker summarized all this beautifully in the following quote:

"Love is what unites. You can feel it in any workshop—the room full of strangers is divided on everything that is a matter of choice, but joined in love whether or not it is spoken. We arrive on its heels, each of us seeking in our own way to recall its warmth, and we leave in its care. It is the full unadulterated truth of our shared vocabulary. The family constellations do not conjure up love; they allow it to be heard no matter who or what has been invested in silencing it; they invite it to be seen no matter how long it has been hidden; they account for it even when the world forbids it; and they remember what the heart sometimes cannot" (Tucker, 2005, p. 20).

Until recently the stories I discovered of my ancestors had been meaningful but in some way still poignant fictions. My ancestors were people I had at last begun to appreciate from afar—something the mind could contemplate but the heart could not yet remember. Then two months ago I found my mind turning to thoughts of Hannah as I sat in the Munich Airport waiting to return to New York City from training in Austria with Hellinger. Hannah's family was said to be originally from Germany. As I remembered her long and dangerous journey to and across America, I had a new sense now of what she had to leave behind. And as I found myself being gently drawn by the deeper currents, tears of gratitude filled my eyes. For the first time I was able to say to her, "I am your great-great-granddaughter. Life went on. Thank you."

References

Benjamin, J. (1988). *The bonds of love*. New York: Pantheon.

Crawford, J. (1996). The severed self: Gender as trauma. In: Arnold Goldberg (ed.), *Basic ideas reconsidered*. (pp. 269–284). Hillsdale, NJ: The Atlantic Press.

Crawford, J. (2005). The delicacy of being. In: M. Weiner, P. Cooper & C. Barbre (eds.), *Psychotherapy and religion: Many paths, one journey*. (pp. 77–103). Lanham, MD: Jason Aronson.

Crawford, J. (2010, January). Poems. *The Knowing Field: International Constellations Journal,* London, pp. 68–69.

Hellinger, B. (1998). *Love's hidden symmetry: What makes love work in relationships*. Phoenix, AZ: Zeig, Tucker & Theisen.

Hellinger, B. (2000). *Love's own truths: Bonding and balancing in close relationships,* Phoenix, AZ: Zeig, Tucker & Theisen.

Hellinger, B. (2008): *Rising in love: A philosophy of being*. (Angelika Schenk, trans.) Berchtesgaden: Germany: Hellinger Publications.

Hellinger, B. (2009). *Success in life: Success in business.* Berchtesgaden, Germany: Hellinger Publications.

Laszlo, E. (2009). *The Akashic experience: Science and the cosmic memory field.* Rochester, VT: Inner Traditions.

Levine, P. (1997). *Waking the Tiger: Healing trauma.* Berkeley: North Atlantic Books.

Levine, P. (2005). *Healing trauma.* Boulder, CO: Sounds True.

Love, B. (ed.) (2006). *Feminists who changed America 1963–1975.* Urbana: University of Illinois Press.

Ruppert, F. (2008). *Trauma, bonding and family constellations.* Somerset, England: Green Balloon Publishing.

Sheldrake, R. (1981). *A new science of life.* Los Angeles: J.P. Tarcher.

Siegel, D. J. (1999). *The developing mind.* New York: Guilford Press.

Stern, D. N. (1985). *The interpersonal world of the infant.* New York: Basic Books.

Tucker, S. (2005). The weight of words. In J.E. Lynch and S. Tucker (eds.). *Messengers of Healing: The family constellations of Bert Hellinger through the eyes of a new generation of practitioners.* (pp. 7–21). Phoenix, AZ: Zeig, Tucker & Theisen.

(As) If I Had a Choice

3

BEVERLY FAUMAN

My journey began some 20 years before I was born. It had always been my father's dream to become a doctor. My father, his mother's second son, was clearly academically gifted, and was favored by her for this. She thought he could do anything he wanted to, and he believed her. Despite significant discrimination in education for Jews in Poland in the early part of the 20th century, he had received a scholarship to high school in a large city near the town where he lived. His father and older brother had already immigrated to the United States in hopes of finding work that would enable them to bring the rest of the family there as quickly as they could, in order to escape the pogroms that were making lives difficult for Jews in Eastern Europe. However, World War I broke out and prevented communication between my grandfather and his wife, who was left with seven children in Poland, and no means to feed them. For the next several years, my father and his siblings subsisted on whatever they could forage, while he completed high school. Finally, the war ended and the family was reunited in Michigan in 1921. My father spoke no English. The practice at that time for school-age children (my dad was 17) was to place them in an elementary school class where they would hopefully learn English while also learning geography, history, math, and science. He was placed in a fifth grade class. Over the next two years, he not only mastered English, but began to plan to attend college and medical school. He did attend college, graduating with a degree in chemistry, and began medical school. He encountered American discrimination this time; Jews had to achieve a higher grade point average in order to continue in medical school, and after the first year he had to leave. He put away his books and his dreams, and had a successful career as a businessman, but he never really recovered from the disappointment of not completing medical school.

As a very young child, I discovered my father's copy of *Gray's Anatomy*, which he kept in the back of his closet. I secretly poured through it, fascinated by the drawings, the descriptions of diseases, and the explanations. I determined, somewhere around the age of seven, that I was going to be a doctor.

I got a little taste of the discrimination my father had experienced. When I expressed my ambition in school or in public, I was often "corrected" that a girl healer was called a nurse, not a doctor. I knew better. And my father, who was a curious mix of Old World and New, never discouraged my hopes. Even though he didn't believe that women could drive (his three sisters never learned) he was quite certain that I could become a physician.

My mother also encouraged me. She had also emigrated with her family right after the war, as an 11-year-old. She rapidly learned English, graduating from high school four years later and completing teachers' college by the age of 18. After teaching for a number of years, she and my father worked in business together. She was proud of her accomplishments, and felt that she had raised an independent daughter of whom she was also quite proud. I also had an older and a younger brother, both ambitious, both of whom did well in school.

I didn't realize how independent I would need to be. My mother became ill during my senior year of high school. Quite abruptly she changed from a very competent woman to an invalid. No one seemed to know what was going on, including the prominent neurologist who saw her monthly for seven months before her brain tumor became large enough to be diagnosed. She died four days post-operatively. During the months she was ill, I was increasingly responsible for my younger brother, as well as for helping out in the family business. When she died, I idealistically vowed to become a better doctor than the ones who treated her. In my senior yearbook, I listed my ambition as neurosurgeon.

My father was bereft. Neither my brothers nor I ever engaged in any meaningful discussions about my mother's death, and we all experienced significant sequelae. Although we have each been successful in our lives, we all bear scars from that experience.

I started college eight months later, still quite raw from her death, and missing the opportunity to share my successes with her. My older brother stepped into the breach, sending me care packages and clippings of my favorite newspaper columns that weren't available at college (Erma Bombeck and Art Buchwald). He had finished college intending to join the family business. My father was firm: he hadn't struggled so hard to see his son become simply a businessman. And so my brother started medical school. Interestingly, my brother tried to discourage me from the same career. He didn't find the (few) women in his class particularly feminine, and blamed medical education for that. His attitude about women in medicine only increased my determination to become a doctor. My plan was no longer to become a neurosurgeon; I now intended to be an internist. My interests and my performance in psychiatry should have told me this was where I belonged, but it seemed too easy. I had no idea psychiatry was not so easy for many medical students. I finished medical school, by now married and with a three-year-old son, and started a residency in internal medicine.

Halfway through the first year of my residency, my husband declared he could not continue to support me (emotionally) in the way I needed as a physician, working unbelievable hours and dealing with life-and-death issues. He moved out. I actually offered to quit medicine if that would appease him, although I don't think I would really have gone through with that. My chairman, an exemplary teacher and physician named Hyman Zimmerman, M.D., suggested instead that I take two weeks off to consider that impulsive decision, and almost as an afterthought on my way out of his office, we exchanged ideas that have had a profound effect on the rest of my life. I said, as I got to the door, that it was too bad there wasn't some way to do internship "part-time." And he said, as I was leaving, "Have you thought about talking to someone professionally?" I was startled by his suggestion. I was healthy, not mentally ill. I couldn't imagine what a "professional" could tell me that I didn't already know. But I also knew that I had never come to terms with the fact that I was "emancipated" at the age of 15, with my mother's illness and death. So, for the first time, I experienced healing of a very different sort.

I saw a psychiatrist briefly, and experienced surprising relief. He listened, nodded at all the right places, and offered sleep medication. He was a trained psychoanalyst, but clearly was able to practice brief therapy, pharmacology, and be a real, empathic presence. After two weeks of leave, I returned to speak with my chairman, thinking I was coming in to take an extended leave or resign. I didn't know how I would be able to take care of my son and still negotiate night call. Before I could say anything, he told me "It is arranged!" What he had done was consult with my internship cohort, asking if any of them had any objection to taking me off the night call schedule—in return, I would extend my internship an additional few months. They were all in agreement. And remember, this was in the days when there were very few female medical students and house officers. To this day, I have found myself looking for flexible alternatives for the house officers I train, supervise, and treat; my version of "paying it forward."

I completed internship, ended my marriage, and took a research position in Gastroenterology for a year so that my son would be starting school by the time I resumed my training. The group I worked with was energetic, with several prominent members including the editor of the *New England Journal of Medicine*, Dr. Franz Ingelfinger. I found the work quite stimulating. However, at case conferences I was often the one to speak up about the patient's possible depression, or self-destructive lifestyle. Dr. Ingelfinger would look across the room at me after a patient had been presented and, in a very good-natured way, say, "And what does our psychiatrist have to add here?" I began to consider psychiatry as a serious choice, but still reluctantly. I thought I would miss the satisfaction of starting IVs and central lines, the success of a good spinal tap, the ability to do a gastroscopy or liver biopsy. On the other hand, I wouldn't be in the position of having to stay at the hospital unpredictable hours longer to work up a "fever of unknown origin."

At the time, residency positions were negotiated individually; that is, the national "Match" for all residency positions was not yet in place. I was offered a position everywhere I applied. I still was sorry to be leaving internal medicine. One month into residency in psychiatry, I realized what a special field this was. We were assigned two patients within our first week, which would hopefully be long-term therapy cases. One of them was a young graduate student who was struggling to complete her PhD, because she was conflicted about whether she wanted to stay in that field. I knew then that this work would be much more satisfying for me than internal medicine was. I had the potential opportunity to make life better for her for decades, while in internal medicine I often found myself doing what I considered piecework, short-term "fixes" for people with heart, liver, or lung diseases. Most of those patients really needed to reflect on their lifestyle choices, and to change behaviors, but in general they were not ready or willing to do that. Furthermore, as an internist, I didn't have the skills to facilitate that. By the third month into my psychiatry residency, I knew I had found my calling. And the night call was every 14th night, not every fourth night!

Over the next few years I was fortunate to have encouraging supervisors, all very different from one another. This was another treat in this field: colleagues seemed to be more interesting and more individual than those I had known in medical school and in internal medicine. Psychoanalytic theory was the currency of the day in psychiatric training; most chairmen (and they were *all* men) were analytically trained.

One of my mentors early in my training, a well-regarded analyst named Dr. Charles Pinderhughes, taught me to be wary if I or my patient thought that therapy would be facilitated, or even easy, if my patient and I shared many common characteristics, for example, being female, Jewish, divorced; perhaps even a physician. In fact many of these apparent synchronies actually can confound the treatment, because assumptions about those commonalities impede an exploration of the specifics. My experience of being female is clearly not the same as everyone's experience of being female; my Jewish background may be markedly different from another person's Jewish history. When a patient says, "You know what I mean . . ." I know to say, "*Tell* me what you mean." When a patient seeks a recommendation from me of a therapist who is Jewish, or female, or Catholic, or Hispanic, I suggest instead that they go to someone I think is really a good therapist, period.

During residency, I met my second husband. He shared my interest in medicine and psychiatry, although he entered and completed his training several years after I did. He had entered psychoanalysis during graduate school. I was intrigued by this: where my first husband had refused to participate in any sort of therapy, this guy actually sought it out, without even being in psychiatric training. Since it was encouraged, at least philosophically by our department, I decided also to begin a personal analysis. My analyst was a Jewish woman, who I presumed had experienced many of the same things I had. (See above!) In that analysis I worked on the loss of my mother so early in my life, the reasons for the failure of my first marriage, and my concerns about being a mother to a female child. I was unsure I would be good at that, still struggling with my identity in what was still a pretty male-dominated world.

My role in the department was interesting. My female colleague and I remained on faculty after we finished training, but were both paid less than our male colleagues who were in the same cohort. Salaries were supposed to be a secret, our chairman hinting to each faculty member that they were getting a special deal which would be withdrawn if we talked about it to anyone. My colleague and I did talk, of course, but felt pretty powerless to do anything about it. We were both assigned as supervisors to the most difficult resident, and were always tapped for women's issues such as consultation to ob-gyn, rape victims, or domestic violence (Fauman, 1982).

I did feel I had some investment in these issues that the men in the department didn't, and wrote and spoke on those topics (Fauman, 1982), but in the same way that I had avoided considering psychiatry as a specialty because it was "too easy," I didn't want to believe that my perspective as a woman was distinct and might be different from that of a man in those areas.

My first faculty position was as the director of psychiatric emergency services, in the newly evolving field of emergency medicine. This was exciting and felt right; my first exposure to psychiatry had been as a "normal" person experiencing behavioral symptoms due to a severe stress. In the emergency department, my favorite role was addressing the emotional responses of patients who came in because of acute medical illness or physical trauma. The emergency resident perspective was to sew up, order labs, and administer meds. I emphasized my belief that there were no "accidents"; I insisted that the residents explore the patient's backstory, and more than once uncovered an intentional or passive suicide attempt in the trauma that brought the patient in. They learned "Don't just *do* something, stand there!"

Once I was established on faculty, at the University of Chicago, my husband and I decided to have a child. This was a very interesting experience, particularly as a psychiatrist. There was very little written on the subject of the pregnant therapist in the early 1970s, (a review of the literature only showed Baum & Herring, 1975; Nadelson et al., 1974; Paluznyi & Ponanzki, 1971) and my very analytic supervisors thought it would be inappropriate to intrude on my patients' fantasies by sharing my news; I was supposed to wait until they asked, and then to analyze their fantasies before confirming that I was indeed pregnant. This was certainly difficult advice to follow; even my colleagues were reluctant to ask whether I was pregnant, so how would patients brave that region? Only one other faculty member in my department was female; the men in the department had various, somewhat bizarre reactions, from being angry, "How many children do you PLAN to have?" (my chairman), to denial in failing to help me identify coverage for my service (the vice-chair), to the advice mentioned above, "Don't tell," (all of my supervisors). Only two colleagues from my department visited me in the hospital after my daughter was born, the other female faculty member and my very first supervisor. I kept notes of my patients' reactions to my pregnancy. One, a schizophrenic who had been in good control for several years, suddenly developed the delusion that our sessions were being recorded, or at least listened to by a third party, within a day after I knew myself that I was pregnant. She left the office abruptly after telling me of the delusion, not waiting for any explanation or confirmation, and never returned. She did decompensate, and apparently took several years to achieve the stability she had had before. Another patient who had developed phobias in childhood after her younger sibling was born took the news calmly, and left our last session before I was going on maternity leave with the plan that we would resume six weeks later. While I was out, she sent me a note saying she hoped I was doing well, and so was she; she no longer had need of my services.

Some patients simply ignored the news, and on my return referred to my absence as a vacation. Dreams and associations let me know they were aware at some level that I had been pregnant and had gone on maternity leave, and I was able to help them work through their own issues related to birth of siblings, their relationships to their own family of origin, and issues that came up for them with coworkers often without any direct reference to my pregnancy, even though it was likely that was what had prompted those thoughts. There is little current literature on the pregnant therapist; as increasing numbers of women have entered medicine and the other healing professions I think it no longer seems a novelty. The most important point about being pregnant while treating patients is to listen for the unasked questions, and to be aware of your own feelings about your pregnancy. In addition, never assume that another woman's experience of her pregnancy is the same as your own. Indeed, no two of my pregnancies have been the same. Treating a pregnant patient requires the same awareness as I noted above; you need to ask, "How is it for *you*?"

I was establishing a reputation nationally on the subject of emergency psychiatry and related issues, such as substance abuse, domestic violence, and the relationship to emergency medicine, when quite unexpectedly, I was courted to be a training director. I had never considered myself in that role, but the chairman who was offering me that position was very sure I would be good in it. At the time, the only female training director in psychiatry in the country was Hazel Mrazek, MD, at the University of Illinois. With my husband, I coauthored a handbook on emergency psychiatry (Fauman, & Fauman 1981) and frankly was getting a little tired of teaching the same material over and over, even though the audience changed every year. Publishing the book felt like I had closed a chapter and could move on.

I found the role of training director quite natural, and enjoyed almost all aspects of the position. I realized that I was now a role model for a whole generation of female medical students and residents; I also felt that I influenced the attitudes of the male students and residents. When there was criticism around the needs of women residents to take maternity leave, I pointed out that I made accommodation for the men in the program who needed to take time off (one with a serious staphylococcal pneumonia, another with recurrent renal calculi), pointing out that the pregnancy of a woman in the program was actually much less disruptive than unexpected illnesses, since we could plan rotations around their maternity leave.

During these years, I began to revisit the idea of engaging in psychoanalytic training. The Psychoanalytic Institute was a strong ally for my residents; from the first, they offered their services as supervisors, teachers, and advisors. They were clear that they should not be regarded only as analysts, but also as psychiatrists and therapists. Some of them were a little nervous supervising residents who were much more educated about pharmacology, since many had trained in the era before the explosion of psychiatric medications. Mutually, they and I insisted that even the best pharmacologist wouldn't succeed as a doctor without learning how to establish a therapeutic relationship with their patients; the analysts also moved towards recognizing that sometimes, medication did make the patient respond better to therapy.

Finally, after the birth of my fourth child, I returned to analytic treatment and subsequently applied to the Michigan Psychoanalytic Institute for training. I spent two years in that institute, reading and thinking about Freud's theories and his approach to patients. My classmates were a very eclectic group: a French Catholic, an Indian, a former physicist, a plain, ordinary Midwestern Protestant, and me, the Jewish voice in the discussion. I think we all learned as much from each other as from the readings and the teachers.

I was unable to continue training after the second year, because I accepted a new job. I became the training director for a much larger program in another city, and couldn't meet the demands of the job at the same time as fulfilling the requirements of the analytic program in the new state. For the next several years I struggled with the new position, finding little to like about it. Finally, my husband and I decided to return to the Midwest, where we had many friends and relatives.

Here I expanded my practice as well as my sense of myself. I began a yoga practice, traveled to several foreign countries including India, China, and Tibet, and on the encouragement of my oldest daughter, who was herself learning some alternative medicine practices, started a meditation practice. During this time, I had begun the most enjoyable and rewarding clinical practice I could imagine; my patient population for the past 10 years has consisted of students, both undergraduate and graduate, in particular medical students, and house officers. My frame of reference remains psychodynamic, although I think I soften it considerably by my belief that patients, particularly the medical students and house officers, know a lot about me. (Another daughter has gone through medical school, her residency, and fellowship during these same 10 years.) Therefore, I am not afraid to express myself by my office décor; I have pictures of places I have been, artwork that I like, and to some extent, pictures of my family. I know that Freud sometimes fed his patients, and saw them while he was on vacation. I believe that no therapist is really the neutral person for whom all reactions by patients are "transference."

Treating college students, medical students, and physicians in training has been quite stimulating. I find most of my patients to be very open to a variety of approaches as well as being interested, in general, in well-being and lifestyle choices. Thus, I often recommend meditation, yoga, or other Eastern exercise/meditative practices, massage, and nutritional suggestions to patients who are receptive to these ideas. I believe that as a female therapist, my suggestions are heard as maternal. The fact that the students are generally very bright and questioning still allows them to challenge me, and to search the Web for confirmation or discussion about those ideas I have put forward.

I believe that my analytically oriented residency training, several years of personal analysis, as well as the years of training in the Michigan Psychoanalytic Institute still inform my practice. Although many of my contacts with patients are brief, as this is an increasingly common phenomenon for psychiatrists, I pay attention to the patient's dynamics, the transference/countertransference issues, and the patient's life story, even in the setting of an emergency consultation. Early in training, I often had the opportunity to treat patients over an extended period of time, sometimes more frequently than once a week. I have learned to "bite my tongue" when I feel the pressure of time and want so much to tell the patient my analytic interpretation of their problem. I learned that lesson in my second year of training, when I saw a patient with a dramatic conversion reaction. She found she suddenly couldn't speak above a whisper, and was sent to the psychiatric clinic after the physicians in the Ear, Nose, and Throat Clinic could find nothing wrong with her vocal apparatus. She told me that the symptoms began in class, while she was presenting her analysis of a book, *The French Lieutenant's Woman* (Fowles, 1969). It seemed clear to me that she found the young instructor attractive, and was upset that he didn't appreciate her brilliant understanding of the book. It was after he made a somewhat demeaning remark to her that she suddenly lost her voice.

Over the next several sessions she tried to justify why she had chosen that book and seemed completely unaware of the multiple layers of sexual content, which are a significant component of the novel, and of the provocative nature of her presentation. By the fifth session I could no longer contain my excellent understanding of the cause of her lost voice, and volunteered it. She yelled that I understood nothing, (her first normal vocalization in over two months) and stormed out of the room, never to return. My supervisor's comment was that I had delivered a premature baby (interpretation); the patient would survive just fine, but it would have been better to wait.

When I first entered medical school, I had no idea what specialty I would enter. I enjoyed internal medicine, really liked surgery, was encouraged to consider orthopedics (a rotation in medical school marked at the beginning by my passing out while watching spinal surgery, and at the end by actually performing an operation, start to finish), and delivered over 50 babies on my obstetrical rotation. While I enjoyed psychiatry, it seemed too easy for me; it also certainly carried a stigma for the practitioner almost as much as for the patient. Bright medical students didn't go into psychiatry.

In the 1960s however, most specialties weren't very welcoming to women. In fact, the only ones that seemed accessible were pediatrics, internal medicine, and psychiatry. If other specialties were more inviting, it is highly likely I would have chosen a surgical subspecialty. One of my daughters is a pediatric intensive care physician, and I marvel at her skills, knowledge base, and the immediate impact she can have on a child's life. I am pleased that the world of medicine is far more gender-blind than it was 40 years ago.

However, when I try to consider what my gender contributes to my being a therapist, I am at a loss. When I discuss patients with my husband, he often has a different perspective, but that is what I was looking for. In other words, I would not have been seeking his opinion if I felt pretty sure about the direction I was going with a patient. I find his comments very helpful, but don't see a "gender" component in them. I also feel that many of my male colleagues have chosen this field because they are also nurturing, "mothering" if you will. I think my gender has contributed more to other aspects of my career development, such as working on domestic violence and rape victim protocols, and in being sought out as a training director.

Being a mother has shaped what I do in the office. From my first child, I learned that children have their own worldview. Having been his primary caretaker for many months, I was startled (and delighted) when he began to talk, to hear his perspective. Not only because he saw the world from two feet up, rather than five feet up, but because he loved to play with words and had his own ideas, he constantly gave me another way to think about things. My second child and my training at that point taught me that children come into the world with their own personality and "stress tolerance." I sometimes find this helpful in treating patients who are discouraged about or disappointed in other people, by asking them how they felt their families viewed them when they were young (Kagan, 1984). They may then recognize that they were often the peacemaker, the victim, the moody one, or "difficult," and, sometimes, then are able to look at their role in their current troubles with a more open mind.

With patients, as with my own children, I am easily reminded that I have no business having expectations of them; my role is rather to help them identify the hurdles that keep them from getting where they want to go. My children may have mixed feelings about having parents who are psychiatrists, wishing sometimes that I could "read their minds," and at other times demanding that I not "analyze" their actions. Some years ago I was asked to consult on a patient on a medical unit, whose depression was interfering with his treatment to a significant degree. We had had a couple of sessions, during which I recognized some of his misconceptions about his illness and his world, but he had not yet come to an awareness of them. I arrived one day to be met with his insistence that he had nothing more to say, and he wanted me to leave. I remained, taking a seat in his room. After a few minutes of his silence, he bellowed: "I've asked you politely to go away, now please be a lady and leave!" I responded that I wasn't a lady, I was a psychiatrist, and I was going to stay. After a few more minutes of silence, he did begin some very useful work, and began to cooperate in his medical treatment as well as become much more appreciative of his wife, who had stayed with him through the illness despite his anger and depression.

One thing I am conscious of: I harbor some of the same stereotypes about females that other people do. Some years ago, my chairman developed a protocol for the handling of rape victims who were brought to the emergency department by the police. One component of this protocol required educating each graduating class of police cadets on our management of those patients. One year, he was unavailable to meet with them, and asked me to substitute. I secretly relished the idea of being introduced to a group of blue-collar policemen as an emergency physician, because I believed they would not expect to see a woman in that position. Much to my surprise, the class consisted mostly of female cadets, the result of a citywide push to recruit more women. And then came my next surprise. I assumed women would be much easier to talk to about treatment of rape victims. In fact, the women in the room were much less sympathetic, even hostile, while the men envisioned their sisters, wives, or mothers being potential victims. From their questions, it was apparent that the female cadets retained the notion that a woman raped was in the wrong place, at the wrong time, and was "asking for it" or could have fought off her attacker. I don't know how many of us revised our stereotypes that day. I know I did.

I would advise a woman considering becoming a psychotherapist to think about her reasons for choosing this field; I firmly believe that you need to know yourself better to be a good therapist than for almost any other profession or specialty. You should appreciate that being a therapist may complicate your involvement in your community, especially if it is a small one; by this I mean that women who engage in treatment with you cannot easily be part of your social network, their children may be in class with your children, you may belong to the same synagogue, church, or temple, you may run into them in a yoga class, all of which can be awkward. Being female does bring something special to the practice. A colleague who introduced me to the psychiatric society in Michigan when I first arrived showed me this in the way she had set up her office. Rather than the spare, "neutral" offices I had seen in Chicago, hers was set up somewhat like a parlor, or sitting room, with comfortable chairs, beautiful artwork and sculptures, and interesting fabrics. Coffee or tea was available to her patients on their way in or out. She knew that there was no such thing as a neutral office, and that patients will assume, invent, or fill in the blanks with their own beliefs. A so-called neutral office may fool the therapist into believing that the patient knows nothing about them.

I know that I have had both immediate and long-term impact on the lives of many of my patients, and that this is a specialty that not everyone can do well. I believe that I have a gift of intuition, heightened by the loss of my mother and the end of my first marriage. My two personal analyses certainly influence my practice. I continue to learn from my patients and my colleagues, as well as my children. I enjoy my work, and am reinforced each time a patient improves. The major stress is that when I am the one a patient has confided in, I find it particularly difficult to take a vacation or attend a conference if that patient is undergoing some distress. A secondary stress is the need to keep confidential what I have heard in the office each day. I have spent many hours seeing patients, but cannot discuss an interesting patient or event in the life of a patient at the dinner table, when we have company or when one or another of my children is visiting. I am not sure I would have gotten as much satisfaction from another specialty, but ironically would not have arrived at this one had I not needed to make a lifestyle compromise early in my career. I would have remained in internal medicine, possibly specializing in gastroenterology. Of course, many gastroenterologists find themselves doing a fair bit of psychotherapy. I feel that as a therapist I have helped not only the patient, but the patient's circle, including spouses, children, and often now, with my current patient population, I think I am helping their patients as well. The fact that your patients entrust you with secrets no one else knows, that you can watch them grow, and that you grow with each patient you see, is immeasurably rewarding.

References

Baum, O. E., & Herring, C. (1975). The pregnant psychotherapist in training: Some preliminary findings and impressions. *American Journal of Psychiatry, 132*(4), 419–422.

Fauman B. J. (1982). Psychiatric intervention with victims of violence. *Topics in Emergency Med*, 85–93.

Fauman B. J., & Fauman, M. A. (1981). *Emergency psychiatry for the house officer.* Baltimore, MD: Williams & Wilkins.

Fowles, J. (1969). *The French lieutenant's woman.* New York: Little, Brown Publishers.

Kagan J. (1984). *The nature of the child.* New York: Basic Books.

Nadelson, C., Notman, M., Arons, E., & Feldman, J. (1974). The pregnant therapist. *American Journal of Psychiatry*, 1107–1111.

Paluznyi, M., & Ponanzki, E. (1971). Reactions of patients during pregnancy of the psychotherapist. *Child Psychiatry and Human Development*, *1*(4), 266–274. DOI: 10.1007/BF01441089.

Psychologist by Accident, Profession by Choice

My Journey of Compassion and Service

4

PATRICIA PITTA

I AM FIVE YEARS OLD AND SITTING ON THE STOOP in Brooklyn waiting for my dad to come home from work. It is Saturday and he only works a half day. That is great for me! Also he stops at the special butcher and brings home skirt steak. I help him cook it. What a treat! As I wait for him I observe the people walking by: some running, some walking leisurely while others are fighting or not talking. Yes, I guess my observational skills began when I was quite young. At family parties when many generations would get together I would watch the interactions. Some were very loving while many were overtly hostile. I come from an Italian/French background so you know nothing is held back. I used to question, "How come people act the way they do?" I made a conscious decision at maybe six or seven years old that I did not want to partake in negative interactions. I would consciously try to act and react in a way based on positive principles and feelings. I guess this was the beginning of my practice of the profession of Psychology. How did this come about that I had this insight? I don't know. Was I born with a sensitivity that enabled me to feel others and be in touch with my feelings in such a way that enabled me to use this gift in a positive manner? I would say when getting my doctorate that I was getting my union card because I was practicing for years.

I came from a very loving intact family with one sibling (an older brother) four and a half years my senior. My parents being first-generation Italian (father all Italian, mother half-Italian, half-French) and children of the Depression, with my father a World War II veteran, they had their share of problems. Mom was forced to move to her dad's home when my father was drafted and that's what accounts for the spacing between my brother and me. I guess for my brother a stranger (his father) appears when he is about three-and-a-half years of age. Then a year later comes his baby sister. Ouch!!! He was the king of the hill. To have to share my mom with his dad and now a baby sister was probably a tough transition. We remained living at my grandfather's house till I was three years old and then the family ventured out to their own residence. My parents' relationship was filled with much love as well as conflict. Most problems appeared to be extended family related. Can you imagine why I became a family psychologist? Boundaries were always an issue that set the stage for conflict. Holidays with the extended family were a challenge that was fraught with tension and relief as they ended. My parents devoted themselves to my brother and me while attempting to separate from their families of origin as well as deal with everyday family and life's struggles. My dad, age 70, was killed by a drunken driver while he crossed the street when on a business trip. He was to retire the next day. He was a fashion designer that afforded him the ability to work beyond 65. The shock to the family was tremendous and I could say my mom never fully healed from this loss. My parents moved a mile from my home a year before my dad's death with the idea that he would retire and be around for the grandchildren as well as to enjoy the fruits of his labors. As a result, I became responsible for Mom as she began to age. My brother has seven children and retired early and moved to Florida. My mom died at 92 years old in 2007. I married Eric Kirk in 1976 and had two children, Eric Jon and Kevin, who are 18 months apart. I received my doctorate degree from Fordham University in 1975. The stage is set for me to be a wife, mother, and professional.

Let's backtrack a moment as I tell you about my education. I graduated from Queens College and obtained a license as an elementary schoolteacher. That is what I decided to become at about the age of five. Upon graduation, I could not obtain a job in the New York City Schools so I decided to go for my Master's Degree in Education at Hunter College thinking I would be able to get a job after completing my degree. I was only 20 years old when I graduated from college, so I had time. One day while driving to Hunter College my car broke down in Manhattan and I was towed to a garage on 10th Ave. and 59th Street. I was told that my alternator needed to be replaced and it would take about four hours to repair. It was a hot Indian summer day in late September. I decided to walk to the first big building that had air conditioning and wait there rather than stay in a hot garage. The first building I came upon was Roosevelt Hospital. After cooling down, I asked myself, "How can I spend the next three hours?" I decided to go to the Human Resources Department and ask for a job. I explained that I recently graduated from college and was going to graduate school and was looking for a job whether was is part-time or full time. I was flexible. I was informed that someone with my background with a teacher's license could apply for a position as a Recreational Therapist or a Teacher in the hospital. They informed me that they had a senior staff member going on sabbatical for four months. Would I be interested in interviewing for the position of Recreational Therapist in the Department of Pediatrics? Of course, I am interested! After four interviews I was hired. I switched from being a full-time graduate student to part-time and my professional compassionate journey began. After four months, the person I replaced returned and fortunately the department of Pediatrics made a position for me as a Recreational Therapist working with children who are seriously ill (heart transplants, leukemia, and working with drug-addicted teens). I found that I love working with the children, teens, and their families. This was the beginning of open-heart surgery for children and as you might expect not everyone survived. I prepared children and their families emotionally for surgery as part of a team including many professionals (Social Workers, Psychologists, Surgeons, Pediatricians, and Cardiologists) and accompanied the child as he/she was rolled in the operating room. During the surgeries I sat with their families and was there for the child as he/she opened his/her eyes after surgery.

I also worked with children struggling with leukemia and other forms of cancer. The journey was similar with this patient population as with the open-heart surgery patients, but more patients died. There was much intense interaction between the identified patient, family, and me. I speak Spanish fluently and worked with many international as well as local Spanish-speaking patients. I found that I loved working with the children and their families. My compassion and understanding for all involved seemed a perfect fit! After working at the hospital for a year I decided to switch my Master's Degree to Psychology. And there you have it, a "Psychologist by Accident." If it wasn't for my car breaking down and my looking to fill hours while waiting for the car repair this road might have never appeared. When I have told this story in the past the usual reaction is that you could have done many other things instead of looking for a job. Maybe it was fate? Who knows? Now let's proceed to my psychology journey!

After completing my internship in Clinical Psychology at Roosevelt Hospital and graduating from Fordham University with a doctorate degree I was employed by New York University Hospital-Bellevue as a Staff Psychologist. I would like to add that my theoretical road began with a behavioral emphasis at Fordham University (Pitta, 1975) and my internship concentrated on traditional psychoanalytic process. My theoretical confusion began quite early in my career as well as my questioning. While working at Bellevue Hospital I performed traditional psychological testing as well as therapy with inpatients. This was an impressive training ground. The level of pathology I saw and worked with was never to be repeated in my career. Working with compromised schizophrenics invested in a paranoid adaptation and the manic-depressives who were quite elevated in mood when manic while overwhelmingly frightened when depressed. The imprisoned criminal who was in the Bellevue jail being evaluated proved to be interesting, yet challenging. I can remember a staff member being trapped by a patient as she walked by; he pulled her hair and banged her head many times on the bar of his cell. The rule was when sitting in a room with an inpatient at Bellevue, sit with your belongings on you, by the door with the door open, and be ready to leave if you feel threatened.

While working with schizophrenics I became involved in research on working with "Language Switching." When a person is upset, even though he is bilingual and speaks regularly in his non-dominant language (English), when upset he reverts to speaking in his native tongue. I had the pleasure of working with Luis Marcos and Murray Alpert on this project. This was my first publication and the beginning of my post-dissertation (Pitta, Marcos, & Alpert, 1978) writing career. After working within the walls of Bellevue for two years I felt the level of pathology so extreme that I needed a more diverse experience. I spent one day a week working at NYU Medical Center within Millhauser Laboratories with a more neurotic based patient population. I was also able to do research. It was the late '70s and there was a real interest on the part of prospective patients to lose weight. The Millhauser Laboratories at NYU received many calls from prospective patients wanting to join weight loss groups. This was the beginning of research on weight loss and its relation to psychological variables. At a board meeting there was a request for someone to spearhead research on weight loss and I volunteered. Since I was 12 I would monitor my food intake and was quite aware of calories and fat intake. You could say I was "avant guard" in my weight and food intake interest. So this was a natural fit. I ran obesity groups and did research on the relationship of anxiety and depression to weight loss. As one would expect as you lose weight your levels of depression and anxiety do get reduced (Pitta, Alpert, & Perelle, 1980). I am happy to report the weight loss program is still active though in a different form now since my beginning this program many years ago.

While at Bellevue-NYU I had the opportunity to meet Sam Slipp, M.D., who was one of the originators of Family Therapy. On a lunch hour once a week I would attend a seminar he would offer to the Psychiatric Residents. I found this type of thinking so embracing that I began training while working at Bellevue-NYU at the Ackerman Institute of Family Therapy in New York City. I experienced the gift of working with people such as Peggy Papp, M.S., and Olga Silverstein, M.S. These people were the pioneers in the field of Family Therapy. So systems thinking became a part of the way I thought about doing therapy from the late '70s. It is important to be aware of how to keep yourself alive and nurtured as a psychologist by learning new ways to think about doing therapy and practicing your profession. One road is to continue your postdoctoral education as you venture through your career.

In 1976 I married which led me to live in the suburbs. This meant changing my job. I don't like change and this opportunity at NYU-Bellevue offered so many diverse professional experiences and means for growth. I drove into Manhattan for a while from Nassau County but after having my first child (Eric Jon, 1978) it became impossible. I really loved working at NYU-Bellevue since I had contact with the more compromised patients as well as the neurotic, and I was able to do research and writing. My fellow colleagues were very invested and forward-thinking professionals. I felt it was the type of position I could have stayed in all of my professional life since there was the ability to grow as an individual and within the system. Going the extra mile you could thrive in that environment which is the way I approach my life. Many of my colleagues stayed there throughout their career but lived in the city or within city limits. Also, many of them were men, enabling them to spend more time with a job while they had a wife at home taking care of the children. So living in Manhasset, New York, I ventured to look at the local hospitals. I applied for a very part-time job working at North Shore University Hospital. I was pleased to discover the head of the Department of Psychiatry was a psychiatrist that I worked with at Roosevelt Hospital. He knew of my work with children and referred me to the Department of Pediatrics that was starting an obesity program and needed a psychologist for the program. It was a perfect fit. This job incorporated my love of children, obesity work, research, and the family therapy interests. I started this job while I was pregnant with my second child (Kevin, born 1980). The hospital was two miles from my home and I started working very part-time (five hours a week). Oh! I forgot to tell you that I started a private practice in New

York in 1978 and I was able to bring many patients to Manhasset, Long Island. In Manhattan I had a part-time practice and most of my patients were willing to travel to Manhasset. So here I was with a part-time job at a hospital and a part-time private practice. It was perfect!

I was able to continue my research at North Shore University Hospital that required I devote more hours to the hospital. Also at the same time my private practice was growing. I can remember when I was 33 years old, one morning I felt like I couldn't get up. I was so exhausted pursuing my varied roles of mother, wife, and psychologist in a hospital and private practice. It all fit in when the children were young. I would go to the hospital in the afternoons when they would take a nap and see patients largely after they went to bed and sometimes in the a.m. (but limited this time to when my husband was home before he went to work). I think you are getting the picture. I never sat for a moment. The job at North Shore University Hospital was demanding more hours to become a full part-time commitment (20-plus hours). My practice was growing. I needed to make some changes. I don't like to leave anything!!! Not my strong suit. I liked being part of an organization. It felt like being part of a family. The reality was that I couldn't belong to so many systems at once (nuclear family, hospital family, and private practice). After much deliberation and working through the proposed loss, I left the hospital position. It seemed a likely move; to have a successful private practice was the goal of the practitioner in those days. It would enable me to be there for my children as they grew and attended school and I could adjust my hours around their needs. So that is what I did. I found that doing private practice and mothering was a good combination, but there was something missing. I missed the further learning and the companionship of other professionals. So I began to look for courses locally to continue my family therapy training. I found one in Suffolk County, which was run by a graduate of the Ackerman Institute. I attended for a year (12 hours a month). Fortunately, I had someone help with the children otherwise my professional interests and endeavors would have been extremely curtailed. I had made the commitment that I would be available to greet my sons after school each day and take them to their activities and just be with them. Well both of my children entered first and second grade. Six hours each day opened up (9 a.m. to 3 p.m.). It gave me the opportunity to further my training in Family Psychology as well as continue a part-time private practice. I started working with Guerin and Fogarty at the Institute of Family Therapy in New Rochelle, New York. This experience immersed me in family systems thinking. I had some difficulty sticking to their only "systems thinking." Working with

Fogarty was somewhat of a relief because he did not leave the importance of the individual when thinking systemically (Fogarty, 1984). When finishing my training at the Institute I felt a yen for integrating the systems thinking with many other theories that I had become familiar with. In the '80s I joined the board of the Nassau County Psychological Association. I worked on various committees and met wonderful people. Some of my need for professional connection as well as giving to my profession was met in this manner. At a meeting I had the pleasure of meeting Gerald Kleiman, who was organizing a Family Therapy Postdoctoral Training Program within a Psychoanalytic Training Program (Long Island Institute of Psychoanalysis). This was again a perfect fit for me. I worked many years in my own analysis and did extensive training in psychoanalytic thinking with Charles Sarnoff (Sarnoff, 1987) who was directly trained and analyzed by Anna Freud. I also kept abreast of the gains in the field of cognitive behavioral thinking (Dryden & DiGiuseppe, 1990; Ellis, 2001). To be able to integrate many schools of thinking with Family Therapy was heaven for me. I worked feverously and willingly to create a course that integrated Bowenian thinking and other schools of thought. I taught for 10 years at the Institute and then the program became less in demand with the onset of managed care taking over the practices in the '90s. There was a direct correlation between managed care infiltration and diminishing requests for Postdoctoral Training. Unfortunately, the Institute closed in the mid-'90s. The local psychological organizations also began floundering with the onslaught of how to deal with managed care that for many practitioners has become "mangled care." Since I was so invested in Family Therapy I joined the American Association of Marriage and Family Therapy and became active on the local board. I rose to the office of President of the Long Island Association of Marriage and Family Therapy. This was a very rewarding experience because the board members and I were very invested in working as a healthy family does and we accomplished having a very effective organization that offered many continuing education programs as well as collegiality.

After this experience I joined the Society of Psychologists in Independent Practice (Division 42) of the American Psychological Association. Many of the board members weren't giving in to managed care and were open to hearing about family therapy and its application to private practice in enabling the practitioner to thrive. My colleagues were writing about how to succeed in private practice without managed care (Haber, Rodino, & Lipner, 2001). Through division 42 I began my writing career on the integration of systems theories with other theories (Pitta, 1995). I was elected as a Member at Large of Division 42. I enjoyed and contributed to the thinking and organizational growth of the private practitioner through working on many task forces that promoted the Independent Practitioner. At the same time I began a relationship with Division 43 (Family Psychology). In the '80s when I was presenting on Child/Adolescent Centered Therapy at a convention of the Nassau County Psychological Association, Daniel Aaroz invited me to look into becoming a member of division 43. At the same time he invited me to consider going for the Diplomate Degree in Family Psychology. I was not able due to family commitments. Our children were growing and their needs were increasing as well as my mom needing more attention after my dad's death. As I grew and matured through the life cycle my interests in the field of Family Psychology grew. In the mid-nineties my writing was ever flowing and my connection to family colleagues began to grow. I decided it was time to obtain the Diplomate Degree. I wanted to be evaluated by my peers as well as seniors in the field of family therapy. I always felt accountability is important to keep a professional "on your toes" enabling growth and self-reflection. Compassion, knowledge, and putting it together were the order of the day. So I decided to venture this process. Of course, it is time intensive and worthwhile because it forced me to present my theory of treatment that became known as "Integrative Healing Family Therapy" (Pitta, 1996; 2005). Also I joined the Board of the Academy of Family Psychology and held several board positions and became President.

What is so special is that being a psychologist affords you the gift of learning about the stage of life you are personally facing so you are able to handle the challenges and pitfalls of the journey of life. I was able to apply Integrative Healing Family Therapy to the Individual, Child/Adolescent Centered Therapy, Marital and Couple Connection, and when faced with struggling with the Sandwich Generation dilemmas I applied Integrative Healing Family Therapy to Parenting Your Elderly Parents. I was asked to partake in making a teaching video by APA publications on this subject (Pitta, 2003). My children by this point were already teens and getting ready to go to college. Time does go by fast when you are having fun.

I need to tell you about my relationship with St. John's University. In 1990 I was invited to join the Family Therapy Supervision program at St. John's Graduate Program in Psychology. I have been supervising since 1990. When Karen Zager asked me to contribute an article to the *Journal of Psychotherapy* in 1995 I felt a bit insecure. Rafael Javier (2007), Director of the Clinic at St. John's, encouraged me to write the article that began my writing on a national level. I thank him for his encouragement and help in this endeavor. A Postgraduate Family Therapy Program was organized at St. John's including faculty from the Long Island Institute of Psychoanalysis. The experience as a teacher and supervisor to students who are your colleagues is a very rewarding experience because you are able to share and grow in your knowledge and further develop your compassion and sensitivity not only as a therapist but a supervisor. Remember when we all started out in the profession the insecurities we feel. What a wonderful contribution to help a future colleague or your peer grow, learn, and help others. The Postdoctoral Program was successful for a few years but the candidates were just not available to continue postdoctoral training. As managed care put its stranglehold on many practitioners they found themselves working longer hours with much more paper, not affording the practitioner the ability to take time and spend money to get further training. After five years the Postdoctoral program ended.

In the early 2000s my work at APA and division 42 became more impossible with my mother aging and requiring more of my help and vigilance. So I had to leave my national work and stay more focused on the home front with Mom's doctor care and illnesses. At the same time 9/11 happened in New York and Washington, D.C. The community where I live is highly inhabited by Wall Street executives. We lost many people in this tragedy. I called the church that day and asked if I could help. The priest told me to come to the mass that night. At the end of the mass the presiding priest asked me to come to the altar and talk to the congregation. I was totally unprepared for this. I thought I would be speaking to interested parties one-on-one. I walked to the altar, maybe a thousand people in attendance all hurting. I looked at the Crucifix and said to myself, "What can I say when there is so much pain?" I talked to the audience about my experience of getting the call that my dad was dead after being hit by a car. After this church experience, I felt this was a signal to become more versed in my faith. I felt it was a baptism by fire. I felt traumatized by this experience to get in front of so many people and being unprepared. But, another way to look at it was that I was where I needed to be to be moved to exploring further my spiritual life. I started to read the Bible with a friend of mine. We would meet weekly and before we knew it we started taking courses in spirituality. We committed to a two-year course in Pastoral Formation that enables you to become a lay minister in the Catholic Church. This was a very difficult time in my life since my mom was declining and I was her sole caretaker. My work in these courses was 800 hours over two years that enabled a great deal of reflection both spiritually and psychologically. From graduation until today I head up the Mental Health Ministry for my parish. I write articles for fellow parishioners combining psychological principles and spiritual tenets (stmarys .edu/social ministry). One of my goals throughout my career was to make "psychology" a household name. I found the way. Teach people healthy psychological principles within spiritual teachings and show people how healthy psychological living and thinking is possible. I write articles for our church bulletin as well as articles picked up by the local newspapers.

In 2007 my mom died at the age of 92—that was the end of a very long-term illness. Having given so much energy to her and her illness, a space of time became available where I could focus on what I wanted to do. My children were launched and my caretaking days were over for now. Three goals had remained: to do court work to protect children in divorce, volunteer on the state level within my profession, and more professional writing. Throughout my career, I was approached many times by lawyers to do expert testimony. That did not appeal to me, but working with so many divorced or divorcing families I saw how parents manipulate the children to serve their needs rather than putting the needs of the children first. The field of Parent Co-coordinating can address these issues with the support of court orders to enable parents to learn to interact with their children in a healthy and constructive manner. I embarked upon getting training to become a Parent Co-coordinator, which involves mediation training as well as Parent Co-coordinating training. This work enables the practitioner to really make a difference in the parents' and children's interactions and types of relationship they have. Also I became active in the New York State Psychological Association and am presently the President of the Clinical Division. My goal was to contribute to my profession on a state level to help the many struggling practitioners with attaining a vision on how they can be effective and survive and thrive as practitioners. I started by giving seminars in Integrative Healing Family Therapy to enable the practitioner another view on how to approach cases by treating the system as well as the individuals within the system. I became invested in running continuing education programs for our members to further open their horizons. I am also the Co-coordinator of Continuing Education at St. John's University with the Department of Professional Development Department of Psychology. With the support of the University and NYSPA the Clinical Division is offering many training opportunities for our members.

Also, this summer I began to write a book which is the compilation of many articles on Integrative Healing Family Therapy. So here I am 25 years later in a very successful private practice, a Adjunct Professor,

Supervisor, Chair of Continuing Education at St. John's University, and continuing to give back to my profession and society at large through volunteering as a professional and as an individual to charities that I have served on their boards for the past 20 years. I did not only serve my patients but I also served my profession by giving endless hours of service to the profession on a local, state, and national level. Volunteering to your profession gives you the opportunity to work for how you want to see your profession evolve as well as aid in your own professional development. You can become a significant contributor and someone who works for the positive growth of psychology in the public's vision and in the profession. It is important to have a vision of how you want to conduct yourself professionally and identify your goals. Of course, in the life of a career, you must change with the times. Another important piece of serving your profession are the interesting people you meet and the deep connections you form which contributes to who you are and become as a person and professional. The profession of psychology has been a gift to me and I know I have served my profession in a most devout and earnest manner.

Many patients over the years have asked me, "Do you act the same in your personal life as you do in the office?" I tell them, "What you see is what you get no matter where I am." I am energetic, dedicated, caring, and an involved therapist as I apply my theoretical knowledge to help patients solve their personal and systemic dilemmas. That means that I will go the extra mile to help someone who feels lost with their issues as well as know when and how to be less active to encourage and enable personal growth as well as put pressure on the system to promote change. I love what I do and to this day the connection with patients is so satisfying and rewarding. To be part of someone's growth is so worthwhile and gratifying that it brings a great meaning to my purpose in life.

Being a female therapist, particularly going through the early women's movement, offered me the ability to become emotionally and financially free to choose my own direction and focus. This journey enabled me to offer male and female patients the opportunity to work with a therapist who changed my role definition, followed by mind and behavior changes in contrast to my sex and cultural background descriptions. Being a second generation Italian American female came with expectations that I met while at the same time I moved beyond laying the groundwork for me to be a woman, wife, mother, professional, and friend with no role models to follow. I felt like a pioneer "trying to do it all" while at the same time building bridges and roads that I questioned if I could navigate. At times, I was criticized for wanting to do it all and not "staying in the kitchen."

When I moved into the community where I lived 33 years ago a woman came up to me and said, "Why don't you quit your job and volunteer with me"! As a result of sticking to my convictions I became more sensitive to appreciate cultural backgrounds and the roles and expectations they assign. A bit of advice for the woman who wants to do it all! You can do it all but if you have major caretaking responsibilities as in child rearing, parenting elderly parents, or a single mother you will need to pace yourself differently. You may be able to reach your ultimate goals but it may take longer than a professional who does not have the major caretaking responsibilities.

The ratio of women to men has changed dramatically in the mental health profession over the past 30 years. Women now dominate the profession. Being a female therapist is a gift to yourself as well as to those people you touch as family, friends, and patients. "We are healers!" So stay focused, committed, listen to your inner voice, visualize what you want to do and how to do it, go the extra mile in any aspect of your profession, and you will be successful, gratified, and do the art you were driven to do.

The journey of psychology is a profession we choose—if by accident, circumstance, or desire—and becomes our choice on how we want to evolve within a profession that offers endless possibilities as long as we have vision, energy, resilience, and ability to adjust to professional, societal, and personal challenges.

References

Dryden, W., & DiGiuseppe. (1990). *A primer on rational emotive therapy*. Chicago, Illinois: Research Press.

Ellis, A. (2001). *Overcoming destructive beliefs, feelings and behaviors: New directions for rational emotive behavior therapy*. New York: Prometheus Books.

Fogarty, T. (1984). The individual and the family. The Best of the Family, II, 71–77. Ryebrook, New York: Center for Family Learning.

Haber, S., Rodino, E., & Lipner, I. (2001). *Saying good-bye to managed care: Building your independent psychotherapy practice*. New York: Springer Publications.

Javier, R. A. (2007). *The bilingual mind: Thinking, feeling and speaking in two languages*. New York: Springer Publications.

Pitta, P. (1975). Effects of token reinforcement on modifying instruction following behaviors in emotionally disturbed children. *Phi Delta Kappa, Universitas Fordhamensis, Abstracts*, New York.

Pitta, P. (1995). Adolescent-centered family integrated philosophy and treatment. *Psychotherapy*, *3*(1), 99–107.

Pitta, P. (1996). Family therapy treatment issues—Family therapy integration. *Independent Practitioner*, APA, Div. 42, Summer, *6*(3), 137–138.

Pitta, P. (1996). Marital therapy: A search for the self and each other—A systemic-psychodynamic integrated approach. *Psychotherapy Bulletin*, APA, Div. 29, Winter, *32*(1), 45–48.

Pitta, P. (2003). *Parenting your elderly parents*. Washington, D.C.: American Psychological Association.

Pitta, P. (2005). Integrative healing couple's therapy: A search for self and other. In M. Haraway (Ed.), *Handbook of couples therapy*. New York: Wiley.

Pitta, P., Alpert, M., & Perelle, I. (1980). Cognitive stimulus control program for obesity with emphasis on anxiety and depression reduction. *International Journal of Obesity*, *4*, 227–233.

Pitta, P., Marcos, L., & Alpert, M. (1978). Language switching as a treatment strategy with bilingual patients. *The American Journal of Psychoanalysis, 38*(3), 255–258

Sarnoff, C. (1987). *Psychotherapeutic strategies in late latency through early adolescence*. New Jersey: Jason Aronson.

From Slave to Midwife
Healing in the Midst of Social Injustice

5

BEVERLY GREENE

> *Make just a ripple, Come on, be brave,*
> *This time a ripple, Next time, a wave.*
>
> —STEPHEN SONDHEIM, 1964

THE LYRICS THAT INTRODUCE THIS ESSAY are from a Stephen Sondheim composition called *Everybody Says Don't* in which the composer challenges the listener to "do," to dare to try, to challenge power, and to have a voice amidst of chorus of naysayers who admonish the listener to be still, silent, and fearful.

> Everybody says no,
> Everybody says stop,
> Everybody says mustn't rock the boat
> Mustn't touch a thing . . .

I refer to the composition throughout this essay because it expresses themes that ran through my childhood and upbringing amidst a group of extraordinary and diverse people. Those themes influence my work as a therapist as perhaps most of my clients are and have been people who belonged to socially marginalized groups. Those who were members of the dominant culture were not perhaps marginalized by society but were marginalized or disenfranchised in some significant way by their families and traumatic experiences during the course of their development. It is fitting that I use musical lyrics to highlight this theme. While none of my family members are or were formal musicians, music was and is still an active part of our day-to-day lives. Prominent Black people who were musical and creative artists were the most frequent visible examples of successful Black people as well as of the creativity and talent within Black people as a group. This was no small thing in a society where Black folk were invisible except in some role serving White Americans. Music can be a vehicle for the expression of complex emotions that words are often inadequate to capture. My paternal grandmother was formally illiterate however could play the piano with ease. I often wonder what her music meant to her and what kinds of feelings she articulated through it, as I now do with words on paper.

The theme of these lyrics captures the message that was at the core of the socialization of children in our family in this generation and in those that came before. That message was about resisting the chorus of naysayers who would respond to life's struggles as well as oppressive circumstances with passive acceptance of the abuses of power directed toward them to the point of disempowering themselves. The message from our elders advocated the strategic use of talents, abilities, and opportunities to advance not only our personal goals but also the advancement of social justice for our own and for others who were victims of social injustice. While we were appropriately warned about the challenges and dangers of racism and other oppressive practices, and helped to develop strategies to manage them both by word and by example, we were admonished to be aware of danger but not driven by our fears. That lesson speaks to the heart of what is often a theme in my work with clients who are members of marginalized groups. It is important to be aware of and assess realistic danger but to also be aware of ways of using one's talents and abilities opportunistically and strategically to challenge, navigate, and negotiate both personal and societal barriers. In simpler terms, this may be seen as learning how to understand the nature of the hand you have been dealt, and how to play it as optimally as you can across a range of situations.

Many of the clients I treat have often been stuck in fear about some real or imagined part of themselves or the world and behave in ways that are not self-affirming but are fear driven.

Helping them to develop a critical analysis of their circumstances, where they may have agency and where they do not, what they are responsible for in their dilemma and what is not their responsibility is also an important component of my approach to therapy that I understand to be rooted in the themes of my own development as a socially marginalized person. Assisting them with strategies is important; however, it is also important to appropriately validate the feelings that result from any encounter with unfairness or abuse, whether societal or personal.

Everybody says wait,
Everybody says can't fight City Hall
Can't upset the cart,
Can't laugh at the King!

I was born in a household filled with adults that was bursting at the seams. There was a wide range of personalities, temperaments, talents, and skin colors that reflect the diversity of Black folk in many ways packed into a two-family structure with three floors on a quarter acre plot of land in a suburb of Newark, NJ.

While we were all Black Americans as family there was great diversity within that group and in retrospect I was given the opportunity to observe the wide range of things that people from the same group might employ to address, in this case, racism and sexism, based on a range of identities and characteristics that also made them different from one another. I could see how the trauma of racism affected different family members differently, depending on where in the South they grew up, when, and how it may have shaped their characterological dispositions differently. It is not a huge leap to see how many of the lessons learned from that group of folks became important elements in my life and in my use of my training and approach to understanding and working with clients in psychotherapy.

Elders: Their Struggles, Their Wisdom and Lessons Learned

I begin this narrative with a story about my great-grandmother and other elders in my family, as my story is an extension of theirs, and the many others who came before me. They have profoundly influenced the person I would become long before I ever knew that I would be a therapist. Talking, telling stories, and attempting to understand how things worked was always important in our family. I contend that I was born into and raised in a circle of particularly powerful healing forces that includes neighbors and community, both men and women. Because race and racism was openly discussed in our circles, it was something I was always aware of. Seeing this diverse range of people who had faced so much adversity with relative dignity, humor, and grace clearly led me to wonder how they managed. While in my early years that question was not so clearly articulated as such, I nonetheless wondered about and asked questions regarding their arrival at certain solutions to racial dilemmas. To my advantage, they were open and shared them. Their capacities and limitations, particularly those who suffered extreme degradation but who did not permit those experiences to distort their humanity, were inspiring. I am similarly inspired by many of the clients I have treated who have suffered enormously but who have a capacity to struggle and avoid permitting their suffering to completely define them. As a therapist, this is perhaps the most fascinating of the processes that I witness in my clients. For many, that capacity to hold on to their humanity despite the many ways they have been ill treated, abused, and dismissed. Research unfortunately does not focus the attention I think warranted on those experiences. Better understanding the formation of resilience in the face of severe adversity is an important challenge for clinicians. It is perhaps easier to dwell on the legacies of misfortune than on the strengths in people who manage to overcome misfortune be it personal or societal who you would not expect would be able to do so. By "overcome" I do not mean they are unaffected by it, rather they do not permit it to dominate their person or their lives. Those individuals who manage to survive and even thrive despite adversity not only warrant our attention but also have a great deal to teach us as therapists as we attempt to assist others who have not been as successful in their attempts to survive adversity.

The Slave and the Midwife

Mary Eliza was a dark brown–skinned woman who was brought into the United States from some island in the British West Indies just after the beginning of the Civil War in 1864. She was my maternal grandfather Dennie's mother. We do not know what her last name was. Those intended for the auction block had no names or any other aspect of their person or their former life that was respected by those engaged in the buying and selling of them. Varying census reports cite her date and place of birth as 1864 in North Carolina despite the fact that she was not born in the US and was in her early teens by the time she arrived here. I always found this ironic as declaring the US her birthplace and setting the date as that which marked her entry into the US as a slave erased all that she was before she came here as well as any written record of why she was here. To be sold as someone else's property. This flaw in the recording of her birth and place also erased the despicable circumstances of her entry that are a part of this country's history that it all too readily denies. We are told that the family responsible for her from the time of her arrival until the end of the war permitted her to marry my great-grandfather, Will Roberson, after the war ended. Initially they settled in North Carolina and then in Southern Georgia. Will Roberson ran a turpentine distillery in Ben Hill County, Georgia, a job that was considered an extremely lucrative but unusual form of employment for a Black man in that era. Most of his peers worked as sharecroppers, manual laborers, or other forms of backbreaking physical labor. A few were skilled tradesmen like my paternal grandfather Thomas, but were often still registered in census reports as "farmers." Despite the desperate times and the privation around them I have been told that Great-Granddad provided well for Great-Grandma and their seven children and that unlike many Black women of that era, she did not *have* to work outside their home if she did not wish to do so. However, she chose to work and became a midwife. In her capacity as midwife she presided over the births of hundreds of babies, including my mother and her younger sisters, and attended both Black and White women in the course of her very long life. This was also unusual for that era. Typically Black midwives would only attend Black women and White midwives attended White women, but she attended both. It was my great fortune that she was still living during the time I was growing up and I was able to spend time with her during some of the summers that my mother, aunts, and cousins visited their birth home in Fitzgerald, Georgia.

Despite the challenges of growing up in a completely segregated society, my mother, a middle child of 12 births, loved her hometown and looked forward to visits there during summers when my siblings and I were not in school. My younger sister and later a younger brother and I were included in these trips that lasted until my grandmother left the South and moved in with my immediate family in the mid-1970s. Aside from being exposed to the blatant racism of the Deep South that was so unlike our experiences in the urban Northeast, we were afforded time with one of many branches of extended family and narratives about family members who were no longer alive. We were able to connect to our family's past as examples of the past of our people as well as to both their struggles and their resilience. Understanding the nature of the struggles that preceded us left in its wake a serious social justice ethos and a sense of responsibility to work for social justice. However it also highlighted the reality that one can be a healing force amidst pain and suffering, personal or institutional, even when you cannot directly change the institutional forces that bring about suffering. It also gave us the opportunity to connect our past to the present, to understand what connected them and perhaps envision what a future might look like. The experience of being connected to something larger than themselves, especially among people who are suffering, is important and comes up in my work with clients frequently. Those who feel isolated and alone in their dilemma suffer more and are less able to see the things that they could do to improve their circumstances. Helping them to feel connected to something is always an important and fundamental piece of the work.

While the range of options available to Black women of that era were few, that Great-Grandma was a midwife never felt accidental. I often thought of her helping to ease the transition of all of the babies, particularly Black babies, that she brought into the world under all kinds of conditions and in the midst of lacking fundamental freedoms for herself. While those degradations were no doubt a source of pain for her, she did not permit them to define her. The attempts to define her as less than her White counterparts did not rob her of her humanity or her dignity and she exercised her power in a very tangible way. The capacity to be a healing force in the midst of misery and pain is one of the most powerful that I can imagine and I have always felt connected to her in that way. It has also had a clear influence on the work I do. In a very fundamental way it is what we do in the therapy relationship.

The last time I saw Great-Grandma she was well over 100 years old; I was 10. Despite her advanced age she was mentally sharp and very physically active. At that time she could still match and surpass me in speed when we walked any long distance. I do not know exactly when she stopped working as a midwife but when she died in 1966 she was, based on anecdotal stories and census records, between 109 and 113 years old. She represents for me and those in my generation a very tangible connection to the Middle Passage and its recency in the history of this country. Her story also represented that of someone who came with literally nothing to a hostile country, made a good life for herself and her children, and became such a healing force in the midst of so much struggle. She played the hand she was dealt and played it well. One of her sons, my grandfather Dennie, was described as a "character" and had many different occupations throughout his relatively brief life. He died when he was just 47 years old. However, for a time he traveled from town to town with a White business partner selling "health tonics" and elixirs. We can only speculate about what might have been in those dubious "tonics" but I often wonder if he wasn't following in his mother's footsteps in some way. The last of my great-grandparents' children, my grand-aunt Irene, died in 2002 at the age of 102.

Another direct link between my family history and to slavery and my sense of healing forces was my maternal grandmother, Flora Roberson. She was the grandchild of a slave, Bella, and her master, Mitchell Tyson.

Her father, Andrew, and his brother, Dan Melvin, were either Lumbee or Cherokee. In her person she embodied a mixture of people who were discarded, disparaged, and whose real identities were distorted to the world, but who was herself clear about who she was and what she had the right to expect from others as what she would have called a "child of God." My grandmother was known amongst her contemporaries as a very spirited woman who loved a bawdy joke and liked to have fun but who was also very spiritual and would share whatever she had with someone in need. Grandma was born in the early part of the last century into a harshly brutal world. I was always amazed that her experiences of loss and hardship had not damaged her enormous capacity to be generous, kind, and filled with joy about what she had rather than misery about what she lost. Her losses were profound and began when she was barely seven years old with the loss of her own mother, Lucy. She delivered a stillborn twin but, unable to deliver the other dead child, succumbed herself. Lucy Tyson Melvin was just 38 years old and the lack of medical care that might have saved her was one of many manifestations of racism of that era. Grandma often spoke of sitting by her mother's bedside for three days as her condition gradually worsened, rubbing mineral oil on her mother's swollen belly in the hopes that it would alleviate her pain. Of course, in the end her efforts were in vain.

Despite losing her mother at such a young age Grandma had great tenacity and flatly rejected the idea that Black folk or women should accept second-class treatment. She was known to openly defy White persons who attempted to cheat or demean her. She stood her ground, even as a child, if she felt she was being wronged no matter who the protagonist might be and challenged people, including White people, if they were treating her unfairly. She and her siblings were often the targets of bullies when they were growing up. Grandma used to tell us that motherless children had a special kind of vulnerability that others often sensed and that it elicited cruelty in some people. However, she believed in fighting to defend herself or younger sibling and on more than one occasion would tell us of sending someone who attempted to torture her "packing" with "a scar they carried to the grave." Paradoxically, there are also many stories about her kindness and generosity. That generosity was what she considered a natural extension of her Christian spirit and exemplified the spirit of being a healing force in the midst of suffering that I have heard people who knew her speak of many times in my life. This is consistent with my own experience of her. I have found those stories to be powerful and inspiring. She could during times that were challenging for her, reach out to others in a way that exemplified being a healing force in the world. For example (Greene, 2008), during the Great Depression many men roamed the countryside looking for work that was usually scarce. They had no money so they often went from door to door and begged for food. She would never turn someone away who was hungry, even when she and her children had little themselves, even when admonished by her neighbors for doing so. My grandfather was dead and she still had seven of their children at home. She once explained to me that she did so because she had grown children of her own in places in the world where she could not be there to help them if they were sick or hungry, that they too depended on the kindness of strangers. She reasoned that she had to hope that if one of her children was in need that perhaps a stranger would help them, but that she must also be someone who helps a stranger in need. While she would not use these exact words to describe her behavior I understand them as her belief that you must *be* the change and the positive force that you wish to see in the world or you cannot ask others to be that force, and that no matter how little you have materially, your person is a location of power and healing amidst suffering. Remarkably, in spite of the grimness of her reality and the hardship that began with her mother's premature death, she did not become bitter, emotionally closed, or so consumed with her losses that she could not appreciate what she had and reach out to others. None of those hardships diminished her capacity to feel for others who suffered while finding joy in her own life.

Like other family members of that generation, there was the message that we all have a power within us to ease pain and suffering and that it is a powerful force that is independent of our social or economic status but is about our basic humanity. That capacity for my grandmothers, great-grandparents, and many others of my elders of that era to be in destructive situations without losing their humor, dignity, or grace was quite amazing; however, their capacity to transform their energy into a healing productive force made them exceptional role models.

In contrast to my mother's experience of her birthplace, my father, the youngest of six, was born and raised in rural Mississippi. After leaving to enter the Army during World War II, he returned only once or twice since in now 93 years of life. His dislike of Mississippi generalized to the entire South so he did not accompany us on these trips with our mother as children. As I child I understood that Dad intensely disliked the South but I was well into my midteens before I clearly understood why. The racism of Mississippi was perhaps among the most vicious in the United States and there is no doubt in my mind that it was traumatizing for him. What was unusual was that although he freely discussed the reality of racial discrimination and its challenges with us, he rarely discussed many of the extreme horrors of lynching or other degradations that he witnessed growing up until my siblings and I were teenagers. By then the civil rights movement and the deplorable treatment of Black Americans in the South was on national television news each night and conversations about his personal encounters with vicious racism would emerge in that context. I always knew my father to be a fair and caring man who had many friends across the racial spectrum. I also experienced him as honest with us about the reality of our being unfairly treated because we were Black (and for my sister and me, because we were Black, smart, and female). Both of our parents stressed the importance of making a distinction between how other people might choose to regard us and who we really were. It is a piece of socialization that goes on in healthy functioning Black families even today. After learning about the abject dangerousness of everyday life for him growing up, I asked him why he never told us about his extreme experiences and how he could stand to work so closely with and befriend White men. He replied, "I wanted you to make your own decisions about people before you heard these things and to understand that not all White people are the enemy, and not all Black people are your friends . . . people . . . are just more complicated than that."

The notion of the complexity of human beings and what they are capable of that goes far beyond their demographics is a cornerstone of my work with clients. While knowing something about their group identifications and their place in the social hierarchy, etc., is critical, it does not tell me how they experience those things. That I must learn from them directly, one person at a time. It was not until then that I more fully understood why my father never accompanied us on summer trips to Georgia and why he deplored the South. What was more amazing was that *he* could see beyond those experiences and maintain a capacity to be open to individuals, even if they belonged to the same groups as people who harmed him. His takeaway message about the complexity of human beings is one that I see manifested whenever I am with clients and in my personal life.

Dad worked as a skilled carpenter for most of his working life, a skill he learned from his own father Thomas. Both of my grandfathers died long before I was born; however, they were both described as very "smart" men who were passionate about their children being educated if possible, but aware and learned. Just being intelligent and knowledgeable as Black men was dangerous in those times. Some might argue that it remains dangerous. They had to underplay their intelligence and humor those who would demean them lest they be seen as a threat. Despite the dangers that could be associated with literacy and ambition, both were important features among my elders.

One of my earliest memories takes place when I could have been no older than three and a half or four years old. My paternal grandmother taught me to write my name, perhaps the first string of letters that formed a word that I had ever written. In those moments, I was certain that I had unlocked the keys to the universe. Sitting in her lap, she would give me a pencil and instruct me as to which letters on the back of matchbook covers made up my name and then instruct me to copy them. It would be years before I learned that my grandmother was functionally illiterate. I watched her correctly sort through the household mail and would have bet you any sum that she could read. I was in high school when I observed her social security check with an X marked on the signature line. When I asked my mother what that was, she explained that it was the mark Granny made because she could not write her name. A long argument ensued between us as I insisted that this could not be so. As someone who is now a scholar I often think back on the irony of those precious moments with her, "teaching" me before I ever went to school, and of course the irony that perhaps my first teacher was someone who could not read nor write herself. For some time and in some fanciful way, perhaps as a connection to her I thought perhaps it was just our secret that she could really read and write but that others were not to know this. Thus in some ways in my work with patients I am a holder of secrets.

As I thought about the people I have described to you I was struck as I often am with how much they did with so little and with so many challenges and obstacles. There seemed to be a guiding wisdom about the way they went about their lives. How they managed has always made me curious about people and particularly marginalized people. That interest in how they accomplished what they did generalized to others who stare adversity in the eye and prevail. Being raised in a crucible of wisdom, hope, and humor has in many important ways shaped the therapist that I have become. Seeing humor in the ironies of the human condition requires stepping outside of oneself, from which vantage point one may have a broader view of the world and of our own dilemma, and I attempt to use humor in that way to help clients step outside themselves to see other aspects of their dilemma and see it differently than perhaps they have become accustomed.

I say try,
I say, laugh at the kings
Or they'll make you cry!

Family Context and Constellation

I am the eldest of four children born to my parents and the only marriage for each of them for now 62 years. Ours was a loving, supportive multigenerational household consisting of my parents, a younger sister, and two younger brothers. We had grandmothers, aunts, and uncles that were part of a large extended family who also lived in the same large house. Our home was filled with books, and pervaded by a sense of humor and playfulness. We were exhorted to think critically, and while we were a churchgoing household, it was driven by spirituality and social ethic more than doctrine. There was an unabashed love for learning and ideas, an ethic to think critically and not simply accept what you are told, and to achieve, but to "lift as you climb." I am often struck by the wisdom of teaching us to view information from people who might have a stake in exploiting us, whether they were White or Black, with skepticism, that there was no substitute for thinking for ourselves. We were also exhorted to remember that opportunities that we enjoyed came from the struggles of those who came before us and should not be taken for granted. It was deemed our responsibility to contribute to the broader struggle, not just our own success. This ethic to "lift as you climb" meant that we were exhorted to assume a sense of social responsibility for the world we live in. This is reflected in my sense of psychotherapy as a tool for social justice and a way that I can contribute to the greater good. Good therapy assists people in ridding themselves of distorted perceptions that they may hold about themselves and others. It also assists clients in being better able to reckon with ambiguity, ambivalence, disappointment, and emotional pain. Similarly, it can be useful in helping clients find the joy in their lives and embrace it without guilt. In the context where social justice is seen as part of our responsibility, my siblings and I were admonished to learn from the struggles of the past of others so as not to have to repeat those mistakes in our own lives. That is also a part of the process of psychotherapy; one can learn from the past and discern how it influences the present in ways that are useful as well as ways that are not healthy. We learn from the mistakes of the past so as not to repeat them.

Growing up in a multigenerational household, we were given great latitude to disagree with viewpoints of adults but to have viewpoints of our own, debate the merits of our opinions, and more importantly to pursue our own dreams and not theirs. Family members also communicated that we had a right to a place in the world, and respect as a human being despite what others might think, and of course owed others respect in return. We were warned that many people did not think much of Black folks and that some even hated us, for no good reason. Such persons might challenge our rights to have the same opportunities that they were afforded and would attempt to undermine us both directly and indirectly (Greene, 2010). Racism was regarded as a barrier but not a barrier that was not to be challenged. Overall, my family represented a wide range of tastes, beliefs, values, and ways of being in the world. I grew up with a clear sense of valuing the experiences and contributions of Black Americans and firmly rooted in that aspect of my identity.

I attended college and graduate school in New York City, very much by choice, attracted to the urbanity and diversity that New York City has always represented as well as a spirit of creative pulse. These were after all, the place where the likes of Langston Hughes, the Gershwins, James Baldwin, the other artists and creative forces walked these streets and left an undeniable creative ethos and spirit. I also grew up fascinated by science with a great interest in medicine; however, I found I did not like the coursework and joined perhaps countless other students in majoring in psychology at first for vague reasons. I entered therapy myself during that period and found the process both intellectually and personally stimulating and satisfying. It further shaped my interest in the therapy enterprise from the other side of the couch. As I developed a greater awareness of myself and what I elicited in others as a person, I came to realize that a great many friends and others confided in me in ways that they did not confide in others amongst our peers. As being in therapy prompted more self-reflection I also discerned that I had a higher tolerance than many of my peers for hearing material that was provocative or emotionally upsetting. It was not that I did not care about the person confiding in me; rather, I could do what I came to understand as maintaining appropriate boundaries between others and myself such that I could feel for what they were going through but did not experience it as though it was happening to me. I grew increasingly aware of my capacities and felt well suited and eager to more formally study psychotherapy. Growing up in the midst of social oppression that took many forms also prepared me in many ways to be a therapist. Members of marginalized groups often have to be bicultural. You must be fluent and equipped to function in the dominant culture while maintaining your own sense of identity. This mirrors aspects of the therapy process. Marginalized group members have the opportunity to more clearly view the dominant cultural ethos or those at the center than those at the center often have of themselves. In some ways this reflects the therapist's position with a client, outside but moving back and forth in a fashion that is not unlike that of moving from wide angle to zoom with a camera.

My public education was unusual. My peers and I were grouped into classes based on academic test scores and there was always a preponderance of Black students in what was regarded as the gifted class. We were exposed to material that was designed to challenge us academically and were regarded as students who were smart and capable with the expectation that we should and would perform well and ultimately go to college. We were expected to think beyond the usual generalities. College took place against the backdrop of the social unrest of the sixties and seventies and New York was a hotbed of protest activity and progressive thinking. I found the demand to place racial identity as master identity to be somewhat stifling. I could not compartmentalize myself in that fashion and did not think it represented authenticity in others or me. Feminist thought, while decidedly not as inclusive as it should have been in representing all women, seemed more flexible and accessible as a place where I could contribute to formal conversations about identity (Greene, 2010). Feminist thought and the mandate to consider social context in working with clients is a central, active, and integrated aspect of my therapy approach.

Everybody says don't,
Everybody says don't get out of line,
When they say that, then,
Lady, that's a sign:
Nine times out of ten,
Lady, you are doing just fine!

Professional Practice, Mental Flexibility, and Optimal Mental Health

Mental flexibility is one of the hallmarks of good mental health. It also includes the capacity to develop a wide range of responses or potential solutions to problems. Good mental health requires the acceptance of imperfection, a tolerance for ambiguity, and uncertainty about oneself and a world that is filled with uncertainty. It includes an ability to both tolerate and view conflict as an opportunity for growth, to have a capacity for connection to other people, a capacity to be open to additional information about the world, ourselves, and others, and the ability to step outside of our own dilemma and view both ourselves and the world through the eyes of others (Greene, 2010).

Lose your "poise,"
Fall, if you have to,
But, Lady, make a noise!

Clinical Implications

My work as a psychologist over the last 25 years has included many clients from many different cultural backgrounds. My training was primarily psychodynamic; however, I found multicultural and feminist theory added an important component to therapy as it makes the analysis of power and the social context an essential ingredient of therapy. In feminist theory, there is an explicit mandate to take the client's circumstances as they are embedded in a social hierarchy of power into account in the therapy process and to help clients understand it as well. In this case, psychodynamic and feminist approaches can often provide a balance in understanding how the social environment has shaped psychic apparatus. I was intellectually drawn to psychodynamic approaches because of their richness and depth, despite the need to revise them so that they are more useful to a wider range of clients. My work with clients has played a major role in the development of my body of scholarly work. Psychotherapy can be a noble enterprise.

As psychologists, we often focus on the individual or an individual as a member of a group and do not give appropriate significance to social context. For feminist psychologists understanding social context is essential to our understanding of behavior. Hence, we must pay appropriate attention not simply to what a person brings to situations, but what the personal and socio-historical context of that situation or dilemma is.

Individuals bring many different dispositions to the world; however, what they do with the hand they are dealt often relies on the availability of social opportunities. It is social opportunity that offers us a chance to develop and express both our capacities as well as distress in healthy ways. I underscore the importance of social opportunity in facilitating optimal development no matter what an individual's personal capacities or background may be. Social adversity also plays a role in the development of both psychological resilience and vulnerability.

My personal beginnings shaped my concern for social justice and my understanding of how psychotherapy can contribute to social justice, one person at a time. Psychological health in individuals can affect our society in powerful ways, as I believe it can promote tolerance and greater openness when people are confronted with problems and are distressed. People who are emotionally healthy have a tolerance for ambiguity. They do not require the kind of rigidity that leads to the need to control others (or oneself) to the point of behavior that is abusive. However, people who have experienced both personal or social trauma can develop more rigid dispositions in the way they approach the world, because for them the world has been routinely unsafe. Helping those individuals to understand and be guided by their painful experiences but not driven or dominated by them is often a task that confronts most therapists. In the absence of the need for characterological rigidity or fear, people can be more comfortable with themselves and their own imperfections as well as with the imperfections of others. Others need not be just like them because they can see the world through the eyes of others while still feeling connected to their own view. Psychologically healthy people also have the capacity to be emotionally present and available in ways that permit them to connect to others and to have a capacity for empathy that makes it more difficult for them to harm or be impervious to the suffering of others. It also anchors them in connections to others, avoiding the pain and the limitations of isolation. Furthermore, having a capacity to feel for the suffering of others need not obliterate the capacity to find and celebrate the joys in their own lives. Healthy people also have an appropriate sense of entitlement. Appropriate entitlement can be viewed as the expectation of fair treatment, having the right to identify unfair treatment accurately, and find it unwelcome whether it can be changed or not. The early lessons from my elders, my professional training, my own identities as a multiply marginalized person, and my accumulated wisdom that is a function of both life and what I have learned as a therapist are all a part of what I bring to the work. I strive to permit my multiple lenses to inform my understanding of clients and their dilemma but always strive for balance so that it does not overwhelm or obstruct my view of clients for all of their complexity and uniqueness.

In the course of my work with them I attempt to meet clients at whatever level of functioning they are capable of at any given time, guarding against the temptation to need them to be better on my timeline and not theirs. I attempt to give my clients the room they need to allow their multiple selves and identities to emerge in an environment where it is safe for them to explore what that means to them, to distinguish between what they have been told about themselves and who they are and what is really true, to understand how to strategically use their talents and abilities to pursue their dreams while managing their realities. I find it effective to elicit their curiosity about how they see the world and why, as well as how they see themselves and why.

Humor is important in life but it is also important in therapy. It requires stepping outside of ourselves and for at least a moment having the capacity to see the absurdity in some of the things we deem so important, that are often based on fears that are an illusion. When I can see clients develop the capacity to laugh at themselves or some aspect of their dilemma I see their progress unfolding. It is a most rewarding process. I have never doubted my decision to become a psychologist. It has been an incredibly rewarding career and my scholarly work has afforded me both a creative outlet as well as a means to voice the concerns of those who do not have the access to voice them. Being a therapist has provided me with the opportunity to be a part of people's growth in ways that mirror observing the excitement of children when they discover parts of themselves or their capabilities for the first time.

> Sometimes you have to start small . . .
> Climbing the tiniest wall,
> Maybe you're going to fall,
> But it's better than not starting at all!

As psychotherapists we can be a part of those healing forces in the world. A large measure of that healing enterprise is found in witnessing and supporting people in the midst of their pain and suffering until it can be transformed into something that helps them become psychologically healthy. The latter contributes to social justice in the world and as such, we are honored to be a part of that process.

References

Greene, B. (2008). African American women, religion, and oppression: The use and abuse of spiritual beliefs. In C. Rayburn & L. Comas Diaz (Eds.), *Woman soul: The inner life of women's spirituality* (pp. 153–166). Westport, CT: Praeger Publications.

Greene, B. (2010). Intersectionality and the complexity of identities: How the personal shapes the professional psychotherapist. In B. Greene & D. Brodbar (Eds.), *A minyan of womem: Family dynamics, Jewish identity and psychotherapy practice* (pp. 452–471). London: Routledge.

Sondheim, S. (1964). *Everybody says don't.* New York: Chappell & Co., Inc.

The Woman Psychotherapist
A Spiritual Perspective

6

MARCELLA BAKUR WEINER

WHO ARE THE WOMEN WHO BECOME PSYCHOTHERAPISTS? At an early age, she became sensitized to the emotional substratum of human life with regard to how people interact and how they feel about themselves, giving considerable thought as to why Uncle Harry acted so strangely and what Aunt Sarah was feeling in her attempts to control the family's affairs. Many who are drawn to our profession were, at an early age, more observers than active participants at home, in school, and in community life. This may have been due to chaotic family situations, in which they felt it unsafe to act openly and spontaneously. Psychotherapists are rarely people who have led armies, built bridges, or ran successfully for public office. On the other hand, they have great acuity in discerning the reasons others have for doing so. Therefore, those who were encouraged to be active participants in the world are reflective as well, wondering about other people's motives and their own. Some came from families that placed high imperatives on self-exploration and social perceptiveness, qualities that require a safe retreat into one's own self. Thus, it is accepted as fact that therapists find the best consolation within their own selves. But, we may ask, why not choose a profession such as "bench scientists" mathematicians or poets—professions that also require considerable solitude and the cultivation of an inner life? It is suggested that those of us who choose to become professional healers do so as the need to cure one's own parents. Also, a high incidence of practitioners is from Jewish backgrounds. Explanations are that Jews are generally known for not deserting their families in times of difficulty but hang in there and try to work things out. If they can't, then they try to make some sense of the misery they are suffering. Both the Jewish and Christian practitioners seem to share these same family values, insofar as none could easily leave their families, even those who had miserable childhoods. People in the field of psychology chose that which is harmonious with their psychological needs, the emotional quality of the parent-child relationship being decisive in eventual occupational choice. Psychotherapists are people who have been cast at a young age into the role of helper or nurturer in their families. This may have been due to being one in a large family, where additional help was critical or because of a psychologically disabled parent. A child in such a family is selected to provide happiness to all; to her is given the role and responsibility of being a healer. Happily, aloneness, or having to care for a parent, becomes transformed to positive experiences. Further, and most critically, children cast into the role of parent, which has to include suffering, is seen as a necessary experience for the practicing psychotherapist. Included is the fact that our willingness to engage in our personal struggle is required for the practitioner's growth as a therapist, as well as a direct resource for the patient.

While the above seems valid for most psychotherapists, especially the women, for me, desire, passion, came about from my being cared about, cared for, and catered to. Probable reasons: as a child, I had been hospitalized for many months, due to an insidious blood infection which invaded my body after a routine tonsillectomy. Not expected to live, at less than two years of age, I did. My mother prayed to God every day in thanks; she, not a very observant woman, who only went to "shul" (synagogue) on holidays, changed her entire routine. My father never went, saying that he observed too many contradictions in men who were observant, i.e., they went to pray but secretly carried photos of naked women. Finding this outrageous, he turned his back on religion, scrupulously observed. Both parents, contrary to the parenting many psychotherapists seem to have received in their early years, were phenomenal: most sensitively attuned to my every need; while non-intrusive, they spent hours beside me, whether in bed or elsewhere, filling me with stories of their childhoods—my mother, Russian, my father Polish, both taught me some words in exchange for my helping them read and write English. My father, having come to the USA after marriage to my mother in Russia, had spent a year in jail, in Siberia, for involvement in political activity to overthrow the czar. On one visit, my mother bribed a guard and they escaped. When they told me this and other such stories, they seemed straight out of the novels I hungrily read about life in Russia prior to the revolution. The only part that saddened me was when the Red Army came in and murdered the children of the czar. Many years later in the USA, when a woman appeared, claiming to be one of the daughters of the czar who, although shot, survived and left her country, I was happy.

In the USA, my father quickly adapted and, by the time I was born, the fourth and last of the children, was a very successful man. The USA had been good to him and he was, fiercely, ever grateful. Money being plentiful, he gave loans to friends, new and old, setting no deadlines for return. My mother, typical of many Jewish families of the old country, was in charge of home and children, spending much time with her prized sewing machine, made all our clothes, my two older sisters and I joyous, allowed to choose fabric, color, and what it was we wished as the new garment. Home was a happy playground.

Though bedridden for much of the time from that early near-fatal infection, until about age five, finally I went to school. Now part of mainstream America, entranced, I loved every minute. In this new world I was "Masha," my Russian name. An early reader, I read every book I could get—my mother or a favorite teacher, my enthusiastic "support" group. Often, my parents took me on visits to their friends, Russian and Polish, from "back home." The only child in the group, I learned some words, listening with total absorption to their stories: life, love, and the Russian revolution of years long past. It was here, in their homes, that I heard the word "God" spoken: with reverence, accompanied by tears, freely, unashamedly, released. My opinion, on all matters, was always solicited as they told my parents what a special little girl they had, her "Russian blood" they insisted, playing a dominant part.

One day, in our home, a close friend of the family, Tanya, had come to visit—daytime and without Max, her husband, never before done. Within a minute she and my mother quickly disappeared into one of our back bedrooms. All I could hear were muffled words and soulful crying, Tanya's. Later, when I asked about this, my mother, sadness absorbed into her eyes and delicate features, said: "Baby, Max has another woman and may leave Tanya." As unknowing as I was of passions and love in adult life, I too felt sad, but only for a moment. Donning my "yet-to-be therapist" stance, I said, in a rush of outrage: "Mommy, why doesn't she leave Max?" Many years later when, as a seasoned therapist, I would hear about a husband's—or lover's—abandonment, I could feel Tanya's pain of long ago, knowing, as I had learned in my years of training and clinical practice, that some situations stay glued to your gut, flaring up now and then, to remind you of life and to be grateful. For, as I now knew, we, having been created by God, are the only ones, number six of His seven species, who use language as our primary means of connecting to other human beings. Choosing psychotherapy as a profession is one most evident example: when having listened intently to the one or ones who have come to us for healing, most selectively we sift it all out, digesting, separating the "small bones" from the large, the inner world, held so tightly, from the outer, spelling out, even at the beginning, what we feel to be the essence of it all: God sends pain to lead us to the Truth. Ultimate joy floods our planet earth, making the sun look even brighter and the moon, more softly luminescent in her quietness. We, the therapist share in this: not, as thought for many years, an emotionally uninvolved professional, doling out decisions, suggestions, based upon the tons of books we have read to become "she" who doles out "life" to our patients, and presumed to be relatively free of all anxieties, all conflicts. When they do occur, it is the patient who has "done it"—the cover known as the "negative transference," all from the patient. Simply put, it is never, but never, we who are at fault—but "she" for is she not the one in treatment? What better proof can we have? Now, I would like to share with you two of my personal experiences: I am senior clinician at a New York state psychiatric center. Having been there for over two years, I am happy: I see the patients who have been designated to me and formed attachments. In general, I am excited about my work, and life as a whole. My colleagues from psychology and social work are most dear to me: we lunch together, share clinical opinions, and know about one another's private world. Life is, indeed, a bubble. One day, I am sitting in my office, reading some notes since I am about to make a presentation. Suddenly a tall woman, unknown to me, appears. Not saying a word, humming softly to herself, she starts to rearrange that which is on my desk: pads, photos of my sons, dried flowers, etc. I get up, gently take her arm, and say: "I'll walk you back to your ward. Perhaps we can talk later." She does not resist. A short time later, I tell this to my two closest colleagues: Olga and Julie from Social Work Services. Their heads thrown back, they are laughing hysterically, barely flinging out the words: "She, dear love, is our new chief psychiatrist." And so she was. Point is—our profession is far from perfect, but when we get satisfaction/ joy/delight by seeing the expression on the face of one person, just one, whose life we have made better, more joyful, satisfying, for their time on this planet, that is our reward, and a large one at that.

When I think now, of the "road I traveled" to become a psychologist/ psychotherapist, some thirty years ago, I realize that, in order to choose a profession, we first have to know who we are: our passions, our attachments, our seeing, our living the "true me" of a "self" that was sent here not only to live for the self alone, but as a human being, connected to all others of this species, regardless of gender, age, color, or religion. I also learned that it is one of the primary commandments in both the Old and New Testament: "Love thy neighbor as thyself." Jesus, it is said, initiated it, Jews have used it forever: when to retaliate against anti-Semitism, Jews, having been made to suffer, sought revenge. But were persuaded by their leaders to do otherwise. Christians too, when they wished to live their "new" faith, were "thrown to the lions."

We have come a long, long way: we offer suggestions, corrections, and right or wrong, we are rewarded: with monies, acclaim, for some publicity of a wide nature, and most of all, the very personal total satisfaction that we have made even one life better, knowing full well, that there is always a "ripple" effect: the "happy now from what I learned in therapy—you'll see, honey, it will be great," from one wife. Or the often encountered: "Well, I have to admit it—I didn't want to go and, from what my friends tell me, most men feel that way—but, boy, she was great—would think she knew me forever." So, now I'm promoted: don't have to go back—and on that note let's celebrate—you pick it, I'll do it. She said I don't always have to be in charge to be a "real man."

Sometimes, there are no "obvious" rewards: no one to sing your praises, recommend you to friends who, when they first see you, say: "I'm so, so glad you can take me. Molly told me what you've done for her. I hope it happens to me." And so it was Marie: I had been working, part-time, at a well-known mental health center in Manhattan. I usually saw patients there. But not this time: Bill, one of the owners, a psychologist, asked if I would make a house visit. To persuade me, he said the "family has money—so, they're paying me well—we'll pass it on to you." I said: "Bill, I've never really worked for the money—but the joy in helping. Give me the details and I'll go."

It was an old apartment building, but had a doorman, so must have catered to "money tenants." and evidently, still do. I gave him a name, he pointed to the elevator, and I saw him then use his phone: he was giving someone my name, but also telling me that: "Marie had been a wonderful painter, pretty well known—well, you'll see it all. Don't want to spoil it for you." I thanked him and went to the floor and room number given to me: the door was slightly ajar. Slowly, I opened it wide and walked in: Marie (I guessed it had to be) was sitting at a long table, dressed in a simple, clean housedress of sorts, hands clasped together, almost as in praying. The room was long, not too large, and, I felt, the only one—to the side, a distance away, there was a bathroom. Outstanding were the paintings on the wall—about fifteen of them, hung in two rows, one beneath the other. I went over to look—they all had a first name of "Marie." I went to sit near her, choosing to sit in the opposite position so as to be able to face her. He hands, smooth, small, were now placed on the table, in front of her. I took one in mine—she did not resist and let it lie there. I said: "Marie, I love your paintings. You are so talented, such an artist." Raising her head, she looked directly into my eyes: "The men are in the forest. There are many trees—the men are hiding there, but no one sees them." One thought that hit me: "It's either senile dementia, some other form of brain damage, or old-old age—older than she looks." All I did was nod and say: "Maybe someone will come and find the men in the forest—and they will have friends." She looked at me and the beginnings of a smile appeared. Her hand was still in mine. We sat like that for over an hour; we did not speak. But, I felt a change in her—the energy level had increased. At that moment, I was more than grateful for the energy work I had been involved in for some years. In brief, energy clinical work entails a set of physical and cognitive methods aimed at developing therapeutic shifts in targeted emotions, cognitions, and behaviors (Gallo, 2002). Energy clinicians integrate non-Western systems of healing and spiritual development into established psychological principles (Feinstein, 2008). My biggest thrill then was, having worked with energy psychology for years with some professionals trained in this, I was given a partner—a woman—to assess her energy—where it was most, etc., etc. Standing in front of her, I passed my hands over the front of her body—and paused—the energy in her belly—big difference. Though new at it, I decided to chance it: "Are you pregnant?" She burst out laughing: "God," she said, "how in the world did you know that? I just told my husband." Of course I was thrilled, finding energy work to be an exquisite accessory in the healing arts.

Whomever I worked with, whatever I did, I felt there was one very, very dependable source: God. The match was always perfect, the learning exquisite. In all of this I felt I was climbing a ladder: the ladder of myself. God in charge, I could, however, go up the ladder, no questions asked or, down the ladder, again no questions asked. My choices always mine still, I knew that I was doing what was planned, for this lifetime. Further, once into spirituality, connected to the healing arts, I was aware that I had had many lifetimes. In one of them I had lived in a society which was vehemently non-spiritual. To silence me, I was sent to live in a cave. Eating plants, drinking rain, I survived. Needing to send out messages about living in Truth, I found an ancient version of a pen, and, using leaves to write on, sent out messages: of hope, faith, and believing.

[She] who knows others is wise.
[She] who knows him(her) self is enlightened."
—*Tao Te Ching* (Lao-tzu, translated by Feng & English, 1997)

References

Feinstein, D. (2008). Energy psychology: A review of the preliminary evidence. *Psychotherapy: Theory, Research, Practice, Training, 45*(20), 199–213.

Gallo, F. P., ed. (2002). *Energy psychology in psychotherapy*. New York: Norton.

Lao-tzu. (1997). *Tao Te Ching*, chapter 33 (translated by G-F. Feng & J. English). New York: Vintage Books.

Transcultural Woman
Healing in a Strange Land

LILLIAN COMAS-DÍAZ

We are all wanderers on this earth. Our hearts full of wonder, our souls deep with dreams.

—GYPSY PROVERB

I AM A TRANSCULTURAL WOMAN—a native and a stranger, familiar and foreign. I live in the borderlands (Anzaldua, 1987), a space full of spirits. As an insider-outsider, I participate in the creation of a new culture out of diverse worldviews. Since I keep my ancestral lineage in my heart, I rely on a syncretistic consciousness—one that allows me to simultaneously hold multiple beliefs, shift from one cultural perspective to another, and integrate several orientations (Sandoval, 1998). As a result, transculturation has infused me with a crossroads identity and branded me as an ethnic hybrid. Certainly, a transcultural woman inhabits strange lands, where dreams feed the soul.

Contradictions curse and bless my life. Born in a frigid land, I grew up in a torrid island. However, my journey began before my birth. I belong to a tribe of wanderers. My progenitors fled oppression carrying a heavy heart. They found redemption in healing. Healing themselves, healing others, and trying to heal their world, my ancestors began a new life in a strange land. Accordingly, I inherited a dual dharma—the need to liberate and heal.

How do you become a warrior and a healer? My foremothers paved my way. They fought against oppression in public arenas and struggled against patriarchal dominance in private spaces. They became healers who carry the banner of social justice and equality. My female ancestors were warrior women who healed with honor and integrity (Achterberg, 1991). The Latino culture facilitated their task. Indeed, Latina healers find in their *curandera* (healer) role a vehicle for resistance against oppression, and a means towards liberation from traditional gender roles (Koss-Chioino, 1992).

My paternal *abuela* (grandmother), Petra R. Comas, was a professional folk healer. She earned her living as a diviner. *Abuela* Petra had the gift of prophecy. She read *barajas españolas* (Spaniard cards), Tarot cards, and auras. Moreover, she interpreted dreams, communicated with spirits, and received prophetic visions. My grandmother seemed to be successful in her business. Predating the frequent flyer programs, Abuela Petra traveled regularly between the United States and Puerto Rico. Long lines of clients eagerly waited at her consulting room in the New York City barrio as well as in the island. Her psychic profession allowed her enough social and financial autonomy in order to become the architect of her life.

My two maternal great-grandmothers were psychics. Family lore declared them mediums. They communicated with spirits in order to foretell the future. Antonia Morales, my maternal *abuela*, was a devout religious woman who invoked the power of Catholic saints in her life. She healed through compassion and altruism. Struggling financially, Abuela Antonia was committed to feeding the poor. My childhood memories include serving food to disenfranchised individuals like Fano, a mentally challenged man who came every afternoon to our home. The daily ritual went like this: Abuela Antonia prepared a plate of food. I took it to Fano, who due to respect, remained outside our door. I waited in the balcony for him to finish eating. As I waited, I relished in the smell of the *azucena* flowers from my grandmother's garden. Afterwards, I returned the empty dish to Abuela Antonia, who then rewarded me with a kiss. Years later I realized that Abuela Antonia used this practice to teach me to be compassionate towards the needy. To me, compassion is a kiss that smells like *azucenas*.

My maternal grandparents nurtured my spirit as I spent most of my formative early years with them. Although they rarely spoke of their Andalusian roots, they enacted their gypsy *duende* every day. Federico García Lorca referred to *duende* as the spirit of the earth, a mysterious force that everyone feels and no philosopher has explained (see www.poetryintranslation.com/PITBR/Spanish/LorcaDuende.htm). He described *duende* as the force that creates radical change, generates unknown sensations, and intensifies life. Simply put, you have to struggle with your *duende* in order to achieve transformation. My maternal *abuelo* (grandfather) Juan Díaz, struggled against rigid gender roles to transform himself into a feminist man. A passionate partner, my *abuelo* worked on a complementary marital relationship where he treated my grandmother with equality, respect, and dignity. Likewise, my grandmother struggled against oppressive socioeconomic conditions. Out of her struggle emerged a desire to live her life with passion and compassion. Every afternoon Abuela Antonia invited me to watch a TV flamenco movie while she ironed the family clothes. As she exclaimed, "*tiene duende*" (s/he has *duende*) at the TV, I longed to connect with my own *duende*.

My parents left their native island with their hearts full of wonder and their souls deep with dreams. The offspring of Mediterranean people and Taino Indians, my mother's Creole physique sharply contrasted with my father's mixed racial lineage. The son of a Black Puerto Rican man and a Creole Puerto Rican woman, my mulatto father struggled against racism all of his life. I inherited a multiracial legacy. As a result, my ancestral DNA tells stories of oppression, wandering, and redemption. Although my face reflects the Andalusian people, Taino, African, and Asian *duendes* cohabit in my soul. While my kinky hair is an African souvenir in the Caribbean, my yellow skin is a testament to the Asian migration into the Americas. With such a heritage, it is not surprising that I became a multicultural psychotherapist.

From Wounded Healer to Warrior Healer

My working-class parents left Puerto Rico and traveled north to soothe the hunger in their belly and the yearn in their soul. Coming from opposite parts of the island, they met in New York but settled in Chicago. Like many migrants, they worked multiple shifts—my father as a factory worker, my mother as a nurse. Mami's place of employment proved to be providential. Physicians at the University of Illinois Hospital recommended an experimental surgery after I was born with a cleft palate. Since my mother worked at the hospital, the doctors offered my parents the surgery at no cost. As a result, I underwent a novel type of operation when I was four years old. Fifty years later, an international cleft palate repair expert at the Mayo Clinic pronounced my operation "a divine intervention" (Comas-Díaz, 2010). The doctor declared that at the time of my intervention, medicine did not have the appropriate technique to repair cleft palates.

Notwithstanding the achievement of my surgery, I struggled for 16 years to "recover" my voice. Having a speech disability marked my development. I turned into a quiet child with an empathic ear. My parents moved from Chicago to Puerto Rico when my brother David was two years old and I was six. This was a treasured transculturation. I encountered effervescent people, vibrant colors, pulsating music, and sweet, pungent smells. Needless to say, the culture shock was intoxicating. However, my parents soon returned to Chicago and took my brother David with them. I stayed on the island under the care of my maternal grandparents. We lived in a two-story house where my maternal aunt Maria Paulina Díaz, her husband, and my cousins Elba and Alberto occupied one unit; and my grandparents and I occupied the other. These were enchanting years. Magical realism accompanied me as I played with my cousins. I learned a new language to translate whispers of pain into cries of joy.

School was a contradiction. It brought the delight of learning, but it also accentuated my broken voice. My stammering separated me from others. Paradoxically, this condition illuminated my dharma. Fortunate in my misfortune, I found in my disability a channel for healing. As a wounded healer, I learned to bond with people in pain—my woundedness spoke to their woundedness. For instance, classmates came to me with their stories of distress. They seemed to find comfort in my quiet empathy. As they unburdened their anguish, I released mine. Being heard is inherently healing. But healing is reciprocal. As you listen, you heal yourself. I decided to become a clinical psychologist when I began healing in a strange land. I discovered that I was not alone in my *otherhood*. Indeed, I found home in an exile community of others. Interestingly, many of my "clients" felt like exiles from their own life. Together we summoned a desire to belong and to be healed.

My exiled family returned to the island when I was nine years old. Their arrival triggered another transculturation. I moved from my maternal grandparents' holding environment to a small farm in the countryside with my parents and brother. During this time Latino traditional gender roles awakened the sleeping dragon of racist sexism. My father clearly preferred my brother because David was a blond, white-skinned boy. In contrast, I was a *jabá* (a female with kinky hair and yellow skin). Papi combated his embattled self-esteem with projection and displacement. Certainly, he wrestled his demons in the presence of loved ones. No exorcism liberated my father from his torment. His struggle taught me that instead of fighting demons, I needed to make peace with them.

As a consequence, I learned painful lessons about racist sexism. My father's behavior appeared paradoxical. Frustrated that his firstborn was a female, however, Papi promoted my ambition and supported my intellectual development. Surprisingly, there was no cultural contradiction in his behavior. Contrary to the United States, racism and sexism in Puerto Rico do not carry implication of non-intelligence. Indeed, many of the island's historical figures have been mulattos and females. Such experience nurtured the development of my feminist and racial equality consciousnesses. Years later, I incorporated feminist and empowerment elements into my psychotherapeutic work. For example, today I explore the real and symbolic meaning of clients of color's racial features. In particular, hair concerns are so central to women of African descent, that these issues require special attention during psychotherapy (Okazawa-Rey, et al., 1987).

Like my father, my mother's behavior was paradoxical. An assertive nurse at work, Mami was an unassertive wife at home. Her behavior contrasted with that of her own mother, who forged a collaborative marriage. It also differed with my paternal grandmother Petra's behavior. My grandmother exercised her independence by marrying and divorcing several times. Without a doubt, my mother reserved her activism for patient care. She became a superb advocate within her nursing role. Although she was a warrior healer, her domestic role denoted a passive resilience against patriarchy. Needless to say, my parents' power relationship informed my feminist development.

During my adolescence I realized that in order to heal others, I needed to commit to my own well-being. As a result, I embarked on healing my stammering. Since I was a voracious reader, I traveled to foreign lands by reading books from the public library. Out of this activity, I found literary models to mentor me. One of these mentors, the Greek orator Demosthenes, provided a model—he cured his stammering by practicing speeches with small stones in his mouth. To imitate Demosthenes, I placed small fruits in my mouth and practiced reciting poems in front of a mirror. As I healed myself I prepared for college.

My college years provided another translocation. Moving from a small town to the metropolitan area, I found in the University of Puerto Rico a bastion of *independentismo*. Promoting Puerto Rico's independence, this political movement sprung from the island's colonial situation. As a free-associated statehood, the political status of Puerto Rico is a contradiction in terms. Due to the Spanish-American war, Spain ceded the island as a war bounty to the United States in 1898. Puerto Ricans became American citizens in 1917, just in time to fight in World War I, as well as in other United States wars.

Although Puerto Rico has some degree of autonomy, the United States Congress and president have the ultimate governance of the island. Puerto Ricans' sentiments about the nation's political status are intense and are associated with a struggle to maintain their national culture, cultural identity, and Spanish language. Promoting the island's political emancipation, the *independentismo* movement fostered liberation within a sociopolitical and cultural context. My university chapter imparted me with fervent social justice and political activism.

Once more, I encountered contradiction. As the university *independentistas* promoted liberation, many exhibited internalized oppression by being elitist, sexist, and racist. To cope with this situation, I read the work of international authors, in particular, authors of color and authors from developing countries. I found in psychology of colonization (Fanon, 1967) a conceptual means to contextualize such contradiction. Thus, I developed an emancipatory perspective that called for resistance and struggle against all kinds of oppression. As a result, I translated this orientation into a warrior healer identity. Consequently, I acquired a historical and psychological understanding of the sociopolitical context of behavior. Today these perspectives inform my clinical practice.

Becoming an Ethnic Minority Woman

My next translocation left a profound impact in my life. After completing a master's degree in clinical psychology, I moved to Connecticut to work in a community mental health clinic. New England baptized me as an ethnic minority woman and showered me with racism, ethnocentrism, sexism, xenophobia, and anti-immigration sentiments. My culture shock was overwhelming. Nostalgia silenced me. Part of my recovery involved connecting with fellow colleagues to establish the Puerto Rican Psychological Association of Connecticut. This organization became a balm against ethnoracial oppression. A member of our organization, Julia Ramos Grenier (nee Ramos-McKay) studied with Brazilian educator Paulo Freire, and helped us to become critically conscious. In brief, Paulo Freire's (1970) education for the oppressed model fosters *conscientizacion*. A type of critical awareness, *conscientizacion* promotes transformation by enhancing individuals' capacity to critically analyze the causes and consequences of their oppressive situation. Consequently, we used *conscientizacion* in our community, clinical, educational, and advocacy roles.

Critical consciousness became a compass in my healing voyage. This model helped me to incorporate liberation elements into a gender-specific and multicultural psychotherapy. While struggling with oppression, I continued to solidify my identity as a warrior healer. However, since colonization imposes an intellectual, cultural, and spiritual hegemony, I needed to examine my internalized oppression. Likewise, cultural imperialism indoctrinated me to develop a narrow definition of the scientific basis of psychology. In other words, I experienced difficulties discerning knowledge from wisdom. Fortunately, clinical practice was the key that unlocked a door. Let me offer you a clinical illustration. During a group therapy session a female client began to channel spirits. Other group members joined in, and the session became a medium séance. What would you do, as the group psychotherapist? Unbeknown to me, some of my clients were mediums determined to help me reconnect with my roots. Partly prompted by this anecdote, I began to study folk healing and afterwards published work comparing Puerto Rican *espiritismo* (folk healing spiritualism) with psychotherapy (Comas-Díaz, 1981). This journey helped me to remember what I had forgotten: A healer heals through her heart.

Years later, I enrolled in the University of Massachusetts (Amherst) to complete a Ph.D. in clinical psychology. This experience was a transformative life chapter. During this period I worked with Bonnie R. Strickland, who helped me develop my psychological research and scientific writing capacities. Her mentoring allowed me to strengthen my scholar-practitioner identity. I learned a new language and Bonnie was my Rosetta stone.

Similar to my Connecticut passage, I joined a Latino clinical psychology group. We worked with students at the psychology department clinic and received supervision from Castellano Turner. Honoring his name, Castellano, an African American psychologist, was fluent in Spanish. We discussed the effect of language, bilingualism, accent, and other linguistic issues on psychotherapy. Additionally, Cass emphasized the relevance of non-verbal communication. We explored cultural clinical issues, assessed the impact of sociopolitical context on mental health, and critically examined the application of Western psychological paradigms to culturally diverse clients.

This experience crystallized my interest in the role of language in psychotherapy. Presently, I work with many clients whose first language is not English. Since there is some limitation when you express yourself in a language different from your mother tongue, I frequently ask clients to express themselves in their preferred language when discussing emotional issues. Of course, I observe my clients' decision to either contain their emotion by using English; or to connect directly with the pain by using their original language. In my experience, following clients' use of language provides a plethora of clinical information.

Later on, I embraced Ignacio Martin-Baró's (in Aron & Corne, 1994) liberation psychology into my clinical work. A psychologist and a priest,

Martin-Baró integrated elements from liberation theology into psychological practice (Blanco, 1998). Like liberation theologians, liberation psychologists focus on critical consciousness because oppression silences individuals' critical voice. Moreover, liberation practitioners side with the oppressed in order to foster personal and social change. Succinctly put, liberation psychologists promote critical awareness, healing, and empowerment, in addition to helping individuals to rescue their ethnic roots and strengthen their cultural identity (Comas-Díaz, Lykes, & Alarcón, 1998).

In my next passage I arrived at New Haven to complete my academic training. Initially schooled in psychodynamic and cognitive behavioral orientations, I received training and supervision from several psychoanalysts, interpersonal psychotherapists, family clinicians, feminist therapists, community mental health clinicians, and an array of professionals. After clinical internship I accepted a faculty position and stayed at Yale University Department of Psychiatry. There I taught and supervised clinical psychology interns, as well as directed its Latino mental health and substance abuse clinic. Working with diverse clinical populations educated me on the value of incorporating multiple perspectives into my clinical repertoire.

During this life chapter I fortified my dual consciousness as a multicultural psychotherapist and a healer. I had previously dichotomized these two identities. Stephen Fleck helped me in the process of integration as he supervised my clinical work. He was a superb intuitive clinician who accurately predicted patients' future behavior. A German Jew, Fleck left his native country just before Adolf Hitler got into power. Certainly, Fleck was a transcultural doctor-healer who helped me embrace my dharma of healing in a strange land.

As I ended a significant romantic relationship, I entered personal psychotherapy. Finding an appropriate psychotherapist was a challenge. I consulted with a Yale University Freudian psychoanalyst, an Australian transcultural woman. She appeared to be an ideal therapist for me. Yet, I found another contradiction. I felt that she did not "see" me. Although her rigid Freudian theoretical framework seemed to be the culprit, I realized that it was her internalized oppression as a woman and as a member of a previously colonized country that seemed to limit her vision. After a tortuous reflection, I did not choose her as my therapist. Fortunately, I found a Jungian psychoanalyst, a White Anglo-Saxon middle-aged man, whose pluralistic perspective made me feel seen and heard. Years later I realized that, just like my paternal grandfather, this therapist was a feminist and nurturing healer. Today I still benefit from his healing gifts.

Understandably, my personal life changed dramatically during this chapter. I married Frederick M. Jacobsen, a neuropsychiatrist of Danish, German, and Cherokee ancestry. A transcultural man, Fred lived in Brazil as a high school student. Moreover, we shared an ardent interest in examining the effect of culture on behavior. We moved to Washington, DC, soon after our wedding. Fred obtained specialized training at the National Institutes of Mental Health, and I became the director of the Office of Ethnic Minority Affairs of the American Psychological Association. During this phase I deepened my knowledge of national administration and political advocacy. Furthermore, I cemented my commitment to global solidarity when I collaborated with the American Psychological Association Office of International Relations in Psychology. This collaboration led me to participate in international mental health fact-findings delegations. For instance, I represented organized psychology in an American Psychological Association and American Psychiatric Association sponsored fact-finding delegation to Chile during the Augusto Pinochet dictatorship. Our mission was to explore the potential role of psychologists in political repression. Based on this experience, I met with the South African Commission on Truth and Reconciliation years later.

Although my American Psychological Association chapter was intense and rewarding, I missed clinical work. As a result, I left national administration and opened a full-time private practice in cosmopolitan Washington, DC. I continued the examination of international social justice issues throughout subsequent chapters in my life. Consequently, I have participated in mental health delegations to the former Soviet Union, Eastern Europe, South Africa, India, Nepal, China, and Tibet.

Seeking, Journeying, and Healing

My journey from doctor to healer has taken me to several diverse places. Integrating my psychologist role into a healer identity has been a significant process. Certainly, clinical psychology training separated me from my cultural legacy. Since cultural continuity is an antidote against anomie and depression (Quinn, 2007), culture shock helped me to challenge cultural amnesia. In other words, I began the journey in search of myself. Even though I traveled around the world, the most important journey was into my heart. Coincidentally, some multicultural individuals translate the term psychologist as "expert of the heart" (Chao, 1992).

To become an expert of the heart you need to reconnect with your heritage. Since I was disconnected from my ancestral roots, I developed a fractured identity. Healing myself required a reformulation of my sense of self. To achieve this process, I had to once more find my voice. Having healed my broken speech, I needed to rescue my spiritual voice. The healing began when I remembered my ancestors' wisdom. Through this experience, I realized that as a *partera* (midwife), my role in psychotherapy was to assist my clients to give birth to themselves.

As a seeker, I realized that life is a learning experience, one where you are teaching, learning, and/or both (Comas-Díaz, 2006). Therefore, my next step was to learn about the similarities between healing and psychotherapy. Both systems share common elements such as the acknowledgment of the role of unconscious motivation, the need for catharsis, and the therapeutic power of working through (Torrey, 1986). Moreover, the two systems subscribe to universal healing components such as the existence of 1) a trained healer whose curative powers are accepted by the client and his or her network, 2) a sufferer who seeks relief from the healer, and 3) systematic contacts between the healer and sufferer in which the healer attempts to reduce distress by changing the sufferer's behavior (Frank, 1973). Of course, there are significant differences between folk healing and psychotherapy, namely, folk healers' commitment to spiritual development. Indeed, a central lesson in healing is the acknowledgment of the existential and spiritual dimensions in our life. Certainly, the development of my spiritual orientation is a lifelong process. Growing up in Puerto Rico, a land pregnant with magical realism, nurtured such development. For instance, although most of the island population is nominally Catholic, in reality, there is a syncretism of Christianity, Taíno animism, African beliefs, spiritualism, and other influences. Growing up in this environment allowed me to acknowledge the metaphysical dimension in life. As an illustration, I believe in the interpenetration of invisible forces into life. In other words, I am familiar with prophetic visions, lucid dreams, ancestor communication, the presence of spirits, and other types of paranormal experiences. The belief in transpersonality, common among collectivistic societies, helped me to make sense out of the inexplicable. This ability transcends the individual self into a self-other-cosmic identity, and thus, recognizes the interpenetration of cosmic influences in people's lives (Scotton, 1996).

The next step in my development was to allow myself to become a healing instrument. Cultural osmosis taught me that intuition was a key to this process. Accordingly, I had an early training: my speech disability taught me to use my body as a medium. Although I had been aware of my intuition, I was unsure of its use in a clinical context. Fortunately, I received validation during my professional training. Boris Astrachan, a professor at Yale University Department of Psychiatry, confirmed my intuition while I presented clinical cases during supervision. Moreover, he revealed that his Jewish Russian grandmother had been a shaman, and thus, Boris was familiar with the use of intuition in healing (Comas-Díaz, 2005). As I mentioned before, Stephen Fleck helped me to integrate intuition into clinical work.

I used my psychological training to learn more about how to use clinical intuition. In other words, I studied the experiences of intuitive clinicians. I found that while psychiatrist Judith Orloff (1996) saw intuition as the ability to allow her patients' feelings to flow through her without over-identifying with them; psychoanalyst Susan G. Lazar (2001) affirmed the use of clinical intuition as being consistent with research findings of quantum physics and thus, relevant to the mutual influence between therapist and client.

In my search I found that Claire Petitmengin-Peugeot (2001) empirically studied psychotherapists' clinical intuition and identified a systematic pattern of usage. Based on her findings she recommended psychotherapists to enhance their intuition by becoming open to this phenomenon, quieting their minds, feeling a connection with their clients, and allowing their sensations to surface without engaging in premature evaluation. Notably, my folk healer mentors taught me to follow a similar pattern. Along these lines, Joan Koss-Chioino (2006) associated intuition with a type of relatedness that healers develop after a spiritual transformation.

Many of my clients call me *curandera* (healer), *bruja* (healing witch), and or *espiritista* (medium) after they witness my clinical intuition. They believe that I can *read* their soul. Moreover, several clients ask me questions about their significant others as if my office is an oracle of sorts. Of course, my clients know that I am no Sibyl. They understand that as a clinical psychologist, I can "listen" to them because they *invite me into their hearts.*

To further my experiential education in clinical intuition, I have traveled to Bhutan, Tibet, Thailand, Nepal, China, Cambodia, Crete, South Africa, India, Turkey, among other places, and encountered non-Western healing practices. Likewise, journeys into Mexico, Peru, Bahia (Brazil), Ecuador, and other places in the Americas helped me to reconnect with an indigenous wisdom. Becoming familiar with spiritual practices helped me to connect with universal energy. However, you do not have to travel the world to achieve this blessing. In my experience, a journey into your heart paves a path for seeking, journeying, and healing.

From Warrior Healer to Liberation Healer

All language is a longing for home. (Rumi, in Barks, 1999)

I found home when I learned the language of spirituality. Definitely, I subscribe to a woman of color's spirituality (Comas-Díaz, 2008). This approach focuses on collective liberation where I see psychotherapy as a service to my community as well as a liberating activity. In this context, liberation acquires multiple intersecting meanings. Accordingly, a liberation healer fights against the conditions that keep people oppressed and enslaved. Like a Buddhist Bodhisattva, a liberation healer commits to collective well-being, universal social justice, and global emancipation. She aims to liberate herself by liberating others. Moreover, a liberation healer attempts to free herself from internalized oppression. Transculturation has served as a vehicle in my endeavor to become a liberation healer. It has fostered my critical awareness, facilitated a transcultural analysis, and helped me to redefine difference as a source of power and self-transformation. To illustrate, Gloria Anzaldua (1987) described a similar process using Aztec mythology. She identified the spiritual awareness, represented by *Coatlicle* or the goddess of death, as the stage where women, immersed in darkness and isolation, empower themselves by confronting their demons. Afterwards, women inhabit a transcultural space—*nepantla* or a land in the middle—where their increased spirituality results in self-transformation. Certainly, this process is analogous to the reconnection with my *duende*—in women's ways of knowing, a passionate knowledge (Belensky, et al., 1997).

Furthermore, my psycho-spiritual development followed a process similar to Tisdell's (2002) model. In studying multicultural women's spiritual commitment, Tisdell documented a process whereby women re-remember spiritual and cultural values and culminate in social action. In other words, women engage in a deepening of their spiritual awareness, honor the life force, strengthen their cultural identity, and, finally, engage in social action (Tisdell, 2002).

Today I am in the middle my life. As an early articulator, I decided against having biological children (Comas-Díaz, 2007). Therefore, I exercise my generative needs through mentoring, nurturing family (both biological and non-biological) relations, and engaging in community service. I participate in psychological associations, cultural and arts associations, and in other community groups. My political and social justice activism revolve around issues of people of color, women, and international human rights.

Middle age is a time to review dreams left behind. To re-remember, I engage in creative expression. My *duende* guides my healing dharma, and helps me accept the strangeness. Additionally, she forces me to re-connect with creativity. The flamenco movies from my childhood continue to play in my soul. Although I have been a healer since childhood, additionally, I was an early storyteller. My cousins circled in front of me as I narrated stories. They patiently waited for words to jump out of my mouth like aircrafts aimed at unidentified stars. Similarly, when my clients tell me their stories of distress, I listen with the same compassion I received as a stammering storyteller. Indeed, healing and storytelling are not strangers to each other. Like streams of water, they cascade into a common fountain.

I associate water with emotions. When I navigate troubling waters, I find myself both lost and found. Ironically, I instinctively know my path. When I arrive to a strange land I invite my *duende* to guide me. In this process, language—my curse and blessing—takes me home. I become a translator, an *interpreter of maladies*—a transcultural woman healing in a strange land. My goal is to translate stories of despair into epics of hope.

If you are considering becoming a psychotherapist-healer, I offer you some suggestions. Be mindful, however, to modify these or any other suggestions to your particular situation. To connect with your inherent healing ability you may want to:

Rediscover who you are
Soothe your wounded healer
Prioritize self-care
Dare to heal with passion and compassion
Nurture your warrior healer
Commune with cultural "others"
Engage in transculturation
Awaken your liberation healer
Express yourself creatively
Embrace your duende
Become an expert of the heart

A Blessing

Becoming a female psychotherapist-healer requires commitment, energy, and struggle. However, the journey rewards you with unique blessings. For instance, you can deepen your connection with yourself as well as with others. Examining your roots and rediscovering yourself constitute integral aspects of your evolution as a psychotherapist-healer. Moreover, becoming a healer is a lifelong journey. As you arrive to strange lands, remember to inhabit the *nepantla*. In this middle space you can meet your demon/angel, or even better, reconnect with your *duende*. Please accept this blessing: *May your journey lead you into becoming an expert of the heart.*

References

Achterberg, J. (1991). *Woman as healer*. Boston: Shambala.

Anzaldúa, G. (1987). *Borderlands, la frontera: The new mestiza*. San Francisco: Aunt Lute Books.

Aron, A., & Corne, S. (Eds.). (1994). *Writings for a liberation psychology: Ignacio Martín-Baró*. Cambridge, MA: Harvard University Press.

Barks, C. (translator). (1999). *Rumi: Selected poems*. New York: Penguin Books.

Belenky, M. F., Clinchy, B. M., Golberger, N. R., & Tarule, J. M. (1997). *Women's ways of knowing: The development of self, voice, and mind*. New York: Basic Books.

Blanco, A. (1998). *Psicología de la liberación de Ignacio Martín-Baró*. Madrid: Editorial Trotta.

Chao, C. (1992). The inner heart: Therapy with Southeast Asian families. In L. A. Vargas & J. Koss-Chioino (Eds.), *Working with culture: Psychotherapeutic interventions with ethnic minority children and adolescents* (pp. 157–181). San Francisco: Jossey-Bass Publishers.

Comas-Díaz, L. (1981). Puerto Rican *espiritismo* and psychotherapy. *American Journal of Orthopsychiatry, 51*(4), 636-645.

Comas-Díaz, L. (2005). Becoming a multicultural psychotherapist: The confluence of culture, ethnicity and gender. *In Session, 61*(2), 973-981.

Comas-Díaz, L. (2006). Latino healing: The integration of ethnic psychology into psychotherapy. *Psychotherapy: Theory, Research, Practice & Training, 43*(4), 436-453.

Comas-Díaz, L. (2007). A psychologist describes her focus on career and the influences of Latino culture. In T. Casey (Ed.), *Pride and joy: The lives and passions of women with children* (pp. 67–73). Hillsboro, OR: Atria Books/Beyond Words.

Comas-Díaz, L. (2008). *Spirita*: Reclaiming womanist sacredness in feminism. *Psychology of Women Quarterly, 32*, 13-21.

Comas-Díaz, L. (2010). On being a Latina healer: Voice, consciousness, and identity. *Psychotherapy: Theory, Research, Practice & Training, 47*(20), 162-168.

Comas-Díaz, L., Lykes, B., & Alarcon, R. (1998). Ethnic conflict and psychology of liberation in Guatemala, Perú and Puerto Rico. *American Psychologist, 53*(7), 778-792.

Fanon, F. (1967). *Black skin, White masks*. New York: Grove Press, Inc.

Frank, J. (1973). *Persuasion and healing: A comparative study of psychotherapy*. Baltimore, MD: Johns Hopkins University Press.

Freire, P. (1970). *Pedagogy of the oppressed*. New York: Seabury Press.

Garcia Lorca, F. (2004, translation by A. S. Kline). Theory and play of the *duende*. Retrieved on July 18, 2009, from www.poetryintranslation.com/PITBR/Spanish/LorcaDuende.htm.

Koss-Chioino, J. (1992). *Women as healers, women as patients: Mental health care and traditional healing in Puerto Rico*. Boulder, CO: Westview Press.

Koss-Chioino, J. (2006). Spiritual transformation, relation and radical empathy: Core components of the ritual healing process. *Transcultural Psychiatry, 43*(4), 652-670.

Lazar, S. G. (2001). Knowing, influencing and healing: Paranormal phenomena and implications for psychoanalysis and psychotherapy. *Psychoanalytic Inquiry, 21*(1), 113-131.

Okazawa-Rey, M., Robinson, T., & Ward, J. V. (1987). Black women and the politics of skin color and hair. *Women & Therapy, 6*(1-2), 89-102.

Orloff, J. (1996). *Second sight*. New York: Warner Books.

Petitmengin-Peugeot, C. (2001). Finding our balance: The investigation and clinical application of intuition. *Psychotherapy, 38*(1), 97-106.

Quinn, A. (2007). Reflections on intergenerational trauma: Healing as a critical intervention. First People Child and Family Review. A Journal on Innovation and Best Practices in Aboriginal Child Welfare Administration, *Research, Policy & Practice, 3*(4), 72-82.

Sandoval, C. (1998). Mestizaje as method: Feminists-of-color challenge the canon. In C. Trujillo (Ed.), *Living Chicana theory* (pp. 352-370). Berkeley: Third Woman Press.

Scotton, B. W. (1996). Introduction and definition of transpersonal psychiatry. In B. W. Scotton, B. Chinen, & J. R. Battista (Eds.), *Textbook of transpersonal psychiatry and psychology* (pp. 3-8). New York: Basic Books.

Tisdell, E. J. (2002). Spiritual development and cultural context in the lives of women adult educators for social change. *Journal of Adult Development, 9*(2), 127-140.

Torrey, E. F. (1986). *Witchdoctors and Psychiatrists: The common roots of psychotherapy and its future*. New York: Harper Row.

The Delicate Art of Connection and Healing

8

CINZIA LEVALDS

FOR SOME, CHOOSING A CAREER IS A LONG, contemplative process that may involve a great deal of vacillation and indecision; for some—like me—the career chooses you. For as long as I can remember, I have been drawn to people and their problems; you might say that I was drawn to suffering. When I was a small child, I was told that I had "the gift of compassion and empathy." I did not know then what that meant; I also did not know the double-edged nature of these qualities. It is not possible, at least for me, to offer that compassion and empathy without also suffering on some level as well. When I first began to practice, this could be overwhelming and consuming; as time has moved forward, however, and I have grown and changed as both an individual and as a professional, this suffering has become more contained. It has boundaries now, and these boundaries, where I once perceived them to be selfish or uncaring, are now one of the greatest tools of healing I have. They allow me to keep the distance I need to in order to see *around* an individual's suffering, while still joining them in their emotional place. I do not leave myself behind to join them, as I did in the beginning; I stay tethered to myself while linked and connected to my patients. This is a tenuous, complicated dance, and, because females are reared with different societal expectations and social norms than males, one I believe more female psychotherapists are likely to grapple with than male therapists.

For women, attachment, connection, and intimacy are, generally, placed at a higher priority than they are for men. In her book, *The Dance of Intimacy,* Harriet Goldhor Lerner (1989) describes it aptly: "Historically speaking, women have learned to sacrifice the 'I' for the 'we,' just as men have been encouraged to do the opposite and bolster the 'I' at the expense of responsible connectedness to others" (p. 7). Since we are women first, therapists second, this is also true for female therapists. In a sense, then female therapists must go *against* their natural grain in order to be the healthiest, most healing therapists they can be, while male therapists may have a head start, so to speak, on keeping that healthy distance.

In high school and college, I was the friend that everyone came to mediate their lovers' quarrels, or to work their way out of their latest personal crisis. I loved this role; I loved being needed in this way, loved being regarded as the person who had the answers others did not seem to have. Every human being has the need to feel valued, to feel special, and this was mine. It was easy for me to see the way out of situations that to others seemed overwhelming, much easier than it was, of course, for me to see the way out of my own. Back in those days, prior to any formal training, I was able to and did cross all of the boundaries that as a professional I would never cross. I would, for example, give my friends direct advice—do this, and then that, and in that order—and I would tell them what I *really* thought, without censor (i.e., "Margaret, you are being completely insensitive and self-centered. You are such a jerk to him!" Think of Dr. Phil, and you get the general idea). There were no worries about conflict of interest, dual relationships, confidentiality, or authorization to release information. There were no boundaries, and at the same time as that was liberating, it also, as one would imagine, caused a lot of conflict, in the form of hurt feelings and broken relationships. Still, all of these adolescent and early adulthood problems were surmountable, even if they were not regarded as such then. They were temporary and controllable, and, contrary to my imaginings, not a good measure of what it would be like to actually practice psychotherapy.

There is a good reason why training to become a psychologist takes 10 years: not only does it take that amount of time to learn and study what you actually realize later is only a modicum of understanding of human behavior—the tip of the iceberg, so to speak—it also gives a person time to mature, have more life experiences, become wiser, *evolve* personally.

When I was in my first year as a doctoral student, my mother, my beloved, nurturing, beautiful mother, was diagnosed with terminal cancer. This was the first experience I had up until this point with a "problem" that was not temporary, controllable, or surmountable, and to say that it changed me would be a gross understatement. My father had died when I was just five years old; my mother raised me, and my three siblings, on her own. An immigrant from Italy, she quickly enrolled in school to learn

English after his death, learned to drive, and found a way to support us. She worked three jobs, and while I did not know it for many years later, we were very financially poor. The fact that I had no awareness of this speaks volumes about my mother's ability to make a warm home, nurture and care for her children, create joy, and teach that joy is a much larger concept that has very little to do with financial security. I learned from my mother that joy is a strange alchemy of—yes, happiness, but also something grander than that—understanding, compassion, connection, and even suffering. I learned that it is impossible to truly recognize joy without first having comprehension of sacrifice. If I have the gift of compassion and empathy, it is because of my mother; she had the gift of attachment and connection. With my mother in the world, I felt safe, anchored; I was afflicted with the magical thinking that as long as I had my mother, nothing truly bad could happen to me. Her presence in my life was like a shield, a protection. When she was diagnosed with terminal cancer, I felt the world as I knew and understood it receding. I did not know who I was without my mother, without the identity of daughter, without this connection to her. When her death came two years after her diagnosis, I had to learn. Moreover, while she was sick, and while my siblings and I rotated time to take care of and stay with her, I began to learn how to accept change in a way I never did or needed to learn before. While I always considered myself to be a spiritual person, this experience expanded this for me in ways I could not imagine, and would affect my practice of psychology in a significant way later. I began to understand that connection is not confined to just earthly things; connection to others is actually the one sustaining thing amongst us. Watching my mother die, and then grieving after her death—all while studying the psychology of human behavior in graduate school—changed the focus, the emphasis, of my study. Ironically, I was taking a class entitled Death and Dying at the time; we were studying Elizabeth Kubler-Ross's five stages of grief. I remember thinking that the way it was explained, in books, in lectures—did not come close to the real human experience of it. It did not capture the flavor of suffering, the catastrophic deconstruction of a person. And it did not explain—not well, at least—how a person went about their reconstruction. I began to wonder if that was the case with all of disorders, pathology, and other human experiences we studied. I knew then that while the training and studying and research were necessary foundations, it would have to be the *connection* I formed with others that would tell me the real story, their story.

Further, I began at this time to see the connection between an individual's physical body and their emotional body. One evening, just a month before my mother's death, I was sitting in the chair next to her at the hospital and we were talking quietly. My mother asked me to tell her about the classes I was taking in graduate school. When I got to my Health Psychology course (a class that essentially focused on the mind-body connection), my mother perked up in her bed, her cheeks beginning to fill up with color in her enthusiasm. "Tell me," she said. "Tell me what you have learned. Did you talk about cancer?" For a moment I was stunned into silence. We tried hard not to mention the "C" word around my mom, even though it was obviously the proverbial elephant in every room. We all knew the prognosis. We all knew what cancer was, what it did; there was nothing more to be said. In those final days, I was using my energy to express all of things I had left unsaid to my mother, trying hard to think of the questions I would want the answers to when she was no longer with me. Her question, and her excited focus on cancer was somewhat surprising to me, but I could see her high level of interest and tentatively answered her question. "Well . . . ," I began, "the research I've seen shows that cancer is correlated with worry and anxiety." My mother's eyes sparkled with life, her voice strong with emotion when she replied, "Yes, that's right. Yes, I can see that." I asked my mother why she thought she had cancer; her rapid, calm reply was, "That's easy. I worried too much. All the time, about everything, and it took this for me to see how unnecessary it all was. I think my body just got tired of working so hard, and it broke down under the pressure of all the worry. Don't make the same mistake I did." She was relieved with her insight; the validation she received from the research seemed to fill her with a sense of peace that is still to this day palpable to me.

I began to wonder if this was true for all physical ailments, that each one had a corresponding emotional counterpart. If some of those emotional counterparts, if unhealed enough, caused proportionately greater physical damage. Years later, this conversation with my mom, and the subsequent thoughts that followed, would be a great catalyst for the population I would be drawn to and serving most in my practice.

I had a supervisor during this period that I came to adore. He knew me just after my mother's death. Part of my training involved taping every session I had with a patient, and listening to these sessions with my supervisors. This wonderful man, during one of our sessions together, stopped our tape, looked at me closely, and said, "Cinzia, you have the ability to attach to others. That is a gift, a wonderful quality that will help many of your patients feel less alone and feel loved." I beamed. It was short-lived. He followed with, "However, your challenge is going to be learning the art of *detachment*, or you will get swallowed and burned out before you even have the chance to reach half of those people that need your help." I watched this supervisor closely; I listened to his accounts of his patients. I found him to be a warm, caring, empathetic therapist—but also one who maintained his distance without the person he was with feeling as though he was not present. Until my mother's death, I could not understand how to simultaneously detach and still stay connected in some way. Having to let go of my mother, and realizing after her death, to my awed surprise, that we were still connected, helped me see the world from a different angle. When she first died, I found it impossible to engage in life; I thought it irreverent and a form of betrayal for me to laugh and participate in life when my mother's presence was no more. I did not see how I could honor her—by thinking of her, by grieving—and also be present in my own life. As I grieved, I learned that it is possible to stay present and tethered to the moment and to life experiences, while—at the same time—staying connected to my mother and my grief. That holding those two emotional places was not only possible, it felt healthier, more balanced.

As I progressed in my career, I found that I could apply the same principles I learned around my mother's death. I could stay present with my patients, while still staying connected to myself; one eye inward, and one eye extended out. I could go home and live my life, and enjoy my life while also thinking of and feeling compassionate for my patients. I learned this the hard way; in the beginning, I felt each patient's energy so acutely that I could almost feel it bleeding into my own; the problem I found was that it *obscured my own energy*. This insight meant that I could not be as effective in helping my patients, a revelation that was absolutely contrary to how I had always thought the process of connection works. I gave myself permission to gain a bit of distance while working with my patients, and somehow found the courage to watch what happened when I did. For me, this was one of the most frightening things I have ever done; my fear was that I was leaving these people, for whom I cared and loved, all alone to struggle while standing by and watching. To me, it was akin to watching a loved one drown, while standing at the shore and shouting for them to try and stay afloat. What I slowly realized was that if I jumped in the water with my drowning patient, each of us without a life jacket, we would both drown. *But*—if I stayed on shore and threw out a life jacket, we would both survive.

While men are taught that holding on to themselves—not merging with another—is standard, expected, women are taught that we are selfish if we do this. It falls under the category of "putting yourself first," something that is considered verboten among many women. As a woman and as a therapist, it is important to understand that not only is considering yourself—taking care of yourself emotionally—*not* selfish, it prevents evolvement and growth if this is denied. It is impossible to know yourself well—and guard against your own triggers as therapist—if you are disconnected from your own needs. Connection to others, in other words, does not mean disconnection from self.

These concepts were not discussed within the context of my training; I attended a medical school, where science, research, and absolutes were stressed. The concept of spirituality did not come up often; it was, I think, considered to be a liability within the psychological context. Psychology is considered to be secular. There was the risk of offending people by talking about spirituality; people are confused about the differences between spirituality and religion; some schools of thought actively discourage spirituality, such as Existential psychology. In this school of thought, responsibility and freedom of choice are stressed; people alone, not something larger than those people, decide one's fate. In fact, none of the basic psychological philosophies—Psychoanalytic, Adlerian, Person-Centered, Gestalt, Transactional Analysis, Behavior Therapy, Rational-Emotive and Cognitive Behavioral Therapy, and Reality Therapy—incorporate spirituality. From its inception, psychotherapy has undermined the doctrines of religion. Sigmund Freud (1961), who is considered the father of psychology, conveyed an aggressively hostile attitude toward religion; he believed that all religious doctrines are illusions and labeled all religion as "the universal obsessional neurosis of humanity." The one exception is Jungian psychology: Carl Jung believed religions to be collective mythologies—not actually real in existence, but having a real effect on human development. Dr. Thomas Szasz (1978) illustrates the difference in philosophy between Freud and Jung in this way: "Thus in Jung's view religions are indispensable spiritual supports, whereas in Freud's they are illusory crutches." Freud argued that religions are essentially evil, while Jung argued that they are imaginary but good. Today, many Christians refer to Jung's philosophies when they incorporate his notions about man and deity through 12-step programs, through inner healing, through dream analysis, and through personality types and tests.

Jung's theories are part of my theoretical framework in practice. My orientation is psychodynamic, which is a less rigid philosophy, with many of the same tenets, as psychoanalytic therapy. Psychoanalysis emphasizes the belief that *all* adult problems are directly related to events in one's childhood. This is the theory that is most often depicted in films and books, what most people imagine when they think of a "shrink." The psychodynamic approach is based on the premise that human behavior and relationships are shaped by conscious and unconscious influences. Each individual is perceived to be made up from a dynamic that begins in early childhood and continually progresses throughout life. Conflict resolution involves individuals healing dissension between themselves and their parents as well as settling conflicts within themselves. The theoretical constructs are made up of the ego (which acts as the balancing umpire), the superego (known as the judge or conscience), and the id (the out of control animalistic, basic part of who we are that rebels against being tamed by the superego). The role of the unconscious is emphasized. A person's successful development under this theory is thought to be the result of managing the psychosexual stages of development. Persons can become "stuck" at one stage or another, and many times where they get stuck is unconscious. This in turn can result in mental distress or illness that may on the surface appear random and unstructured. Psychodynamic theory emphasizes making the unconscious conscious so that insight and healing can take place. I integrate this approach with my own spiritual foundation, exploring not just how a person's past experience might be impacting their current functioning, but also exploring how their current experience can *serve* them. It is my belief, not achieved through formal training but from life experiences, that what happens to us happens *for* us. This includes, in my view, people's experiences, and especially, their traumas. I believe, and practice with the philosophy, that our greatest challenges are our greatest teachers. It is our responsibility to understand and to use those experiences in some way that serves us.

I operate in my practice from the premise that our belief systems are formed early in childhood; some of these, many of these, belief systems are unconscious and negative. A belief system, as I understand and practice it, is a set of beliefs we have about ourselves that form who we believe ourselves to be. These belief systems—what we really believe about who we are—can or cannot be accurate, or be the truth. They can formulate the personality we then adopt, which in turn, may or may not be an accurate representation of who a person actually is. The soul, or core, or truth of who we are, for example, may be—and in my experience often is—different from the personality we end up adopting (usually largely unconscious) through the experiences we have beginning in early childhood and continue to have as we progress through life. Personality development, in my view, is a combination of these experiences, internalizations (what we were told about who we are) from key players in our lives (e.g., parents, siblings, teachers, friends), and belief systems we may have been "infected" by through those key players. For example, a person may come to therapy because no matter what she does, she cannot be financially successful. She may feel that she tries as hard as she is able, acquires good jobs and makes a good salary, but she finds she is always struggling. A deeper exploration may unveil an unconscious belief system that money is dangerous or evil, that those who acquire it pay the consequences in the form of broken relationships: in other words, money ruins people. This belief system may have been an incorporation of a parent's belief system, whereby the patient has been sent sundry messages that those who acquire financial success are lacking in more important areas, that it is not possible to have both good relationships and money. We as human beings have belief systems about all major values, about other people or groups of people, and especially, about the kind of person we think we are.

While I incorporate the basic philosophy of psychodynamic theory, I have found it to be incomplete; I have found it to be lacking in a clear foundation that clarifies the reason for our existence. This is the path of study I chose to pursue after my formal training—that of a spiritual nature. Forming my private practice and doing this work triggered more questions: Why do some people seem to have much easier lives than other people? Why are some people's lives wracked with suffering and stress, while other lives are spared major losses? How does this affect the physical body? What is our purpose as a collective humanity and how do we arrive at this purpose? Are there unseen forces at work beyond our comprehension, a kind of spiritual support and assistance that some people are more connected to than others? If so, how do we strengthen that connection? Does strengthening that connection then, by default, also strengthen the connection we have to ourselves? If so—if we are more connected to ourselves on a spiritual level—does that positively impact our physical functioning?

A few years into my practice, I became interested in doing work with individuals who have chronic illnesses. Multiple sclerosis (MS), in particular, became of particular interest to me. This disease takes on such an individual course with every person who is living with it; the variance in prognosis and progression, even when there are very similar levels of neurological damage, was and is intriguing to me. For this reason, neurologists have a hard time giving patients answers about the course of their illness when they are diagnosed. When I began studying MS, the conversation I had that evening in the hospital about cancer so many years ago with my mother was foremost in my mind. I became, and remain, fascinated that perhaps the missing element in predicting the course the disease takes has something to do with psychological factors, particularly the unhealed emotional parts of people perhaps having a role in the course of the disease. If I could help them heal some of these emotional factors, would they get better physically? After 10 years of working with this population, I can say the answer to my question is unequivocally, yes. The role stress plays in MS is well documented in research; we know that stress can cause exacerbations, or flare-ups, in MS patients, and that chronic stress can negatively influence prognosis and recovery. One of the most rewarding aspects of my work is helping to empower these patients living with a disease that is arguably the most unpredictable one a person can have. When MS patients discover how their negative belief systems can be toxic to their physical functioning as well as their emotional functioning—and that the two are highly linked—they have more choice and power to shift these belief systems, to deconstruct them and then reconstruct them into healthier constructs. When diagnosed with MS, or any other chronic illness, hopelessness can be just an arm's length away. No human being wants to feel that they have no control over their functioning and health. Working with people who have MS has shown me, time and time again, what the power of belief systems can do, in both the positive and negative sense. The truth is that we have much more control than we sometimes think we do—but not in the way we think we have it. The control rests internally; it is not associated with external things, such as controlling other people or situations. Control, in its truest sense, has to do with how we filter information, how we interpret it, and then what we do with that information. How we can use it, to better ourselves and to grow. How we function mentally, emotionally, and physically, is predicated upon how we do this.

In graduate school, on the way to becoming a healer, students will be exposed to all of the theories and philosophies and history of psychology. They will learn what the masters, the giants, have learned, and how to apply it. What cannot be acquired from formal training, what cannot be taught, is one's belief systems, both individual and of the world. All psychotherapists, to be the best healers they can be, must deconstruct their own belief systems, both to understand themselves better and to make sure they are seeing others clearly, that they are not "infecting" others with their own faulty belief systems.

I began this essay with the statement that I did not choose to be a psychotherapist, but rather the profession chose me. This is an incomplete statement, because while I believe that something larger than who we are guides and supports us, I also believe that we have free will to collaborate with that energy, to work with it. Life offers opportunities, but we choose whether to use them. I would choose to the same career path if I had to choose today. It is the only one that I know of where working on your psyche, and resulting evolvement, is a requisite to being good at what you do; it is the only one I know of that shifts and changes you each and every day when you encounter another person's story and observe how they are living it. Psychotherapy is a very delicate dance; you must be alert to your own "issues," so that when you encounter parallels in therapy, you know if and how you can navigate them. As a woman, you must also be alert to the societal norms and mores that you have been indoctrinated with, and how this influences your therapeutic style. For me, understanding that connecting to another person is not the same as attaching to them; you can connect with another but still remain attached to who you are.

Although my theoretical orientation is based on the psychodynamic theory, it must be said that no matter what theoretical orientation a psychotherapist chooses—or a combination of theories—the *relationship* between the patient and therapist is of utmost importance. It surpasses all of the technical knowledge a person may have. In my practice, I operate by this philosophy: Do not work with anyone you cannot love. The reason the relationship is so important, the connection between people, is because it is the energy of love there that actually heals. They don't tell you this in graduate school, but without this, you have nothing. No level of training or therapeutic tool will effect change without the energy of authentic love between the therapeutic partners.

While it still makes me feel "special" to play the role of therapist, a better way to describe it for me today is *honored* or *privileged*. I now understand that it is not *me*, or my theoretical orientation and practice, that changes people, it is the result of something larger than that at work, a complicated collaboration with a strong spiritual component. I am only the witness to others' transformations, not the agent. Only they are. And that is an honor.

References

Freud, Sigmund (1961). *The future of an illusion* (p. 43). New York: W. W. Norton and Company, Inc.

Lerner, H. G. (1989). *The dance of intimacy*. New York: Harper and Row.

Szasz, Thomas S. (1978). *The myth of psychotherapy* (p. 173). Garden City: Doubleday/Anchor Press.

Becoming a Psychotherapist
Discovering the Self amidst Cultural Shifts

9

PRATYUSHA TUMMALA-NARRA

OVER THE PAST TWO DECADES, the gender of the psychotherapist has been thought to be relevant to the therapeutic process. It is particularly important then that the ways in which women psychotherapists experience and influence the therapeutic relationship be understood from the perspective of women (Cantor, 1990). I am grateful for the opportunity to share some of my most salient experiences in the hope of providing a lens into the deeply emotional and transformative life of a female psychotherapist. In reflecting on how I became a psychotherapist, I realize that this process has been shaped through the interaction of multiple layers of experience, both personal and professional. In this chapter, I will discuss how I began my journey as a therapist, how this journey has progressed into developing a framework for understanding the self and culture, facing racism, negotiating life transitions, and some lessons that I have learned thus far which may be valuable to other women who presently are or are becoming psychotherapists.

India to the U.S.: First Journey in Becoming a Therapist

Although I initially considered becoming a psychologist as a college student, I was not consciously aware of the influence of my early life on my professional inclinations at the time. I have since realized that my decision to become a therapist was set in motion long before college and graduate school.

I was born in Hyderabad (in the Southern state of Andhra Pradesh), India, and for the first seven years of my life, I lived with my parents, older brother, maternal great-grandparents, and maternal aunt. I visited my paternal grandparents during our summer holidays. My early memories are those filled with interactions with my family, and of belonging. I was especially close to my maternal great-grandparents who held a revered role in the family, introducing me to the value of respecting one's elders and of the wisdom they imparted. My maternal grandparents left India when I was an infant, and moved to New York City, where my grandfather had completed a part of his medical training in the 1950s, a time when Indian migration to the U.S. was limited by immigration policy that discriminated against Asians. My grandparents moved to the U.S. after surviving political violence spurred by tension between two communities of different Hindu castes. The tensions between the castes were rooted in land divisions at the end of British occupation in India. My grandparents were contemporaries and followers of Mahatma Gandhi, and held strong beliefs in equality among castes and religious groups. The precipitating event for their emigration was an incident when their home was set on fire by members of a different caste. While the fire and its aftermath remain in my family's collective memory of life in India during this time, this incident and the subsequent separations and losses in the following years for our extended family were seldom spoken about.

As a young child in India, I remember a contrast in experience of simultaneously interacting with neighbors and classmates from various religious backgrounds (Hindu, Muslim, Christian), and then observing curfews due to tensions between Hindus and Muslims in our city. My brother and I woke up to the prayers emanating from the local mosque, listened to the prayers of our great-grandfather, and then attended a Christian grammar school. Indeed, our multicultural experience began long before our move to the United States.

My parents decided that we would move to the U.S. amidst continued political tensions in Hyderabad, and we joined our grandparents in New York City when I was seven years old. After relocating to the U.S., my father completed a second residency in the U.S. in order to be able to practice medicine. My mother had dreams of carving out a new and different life for herself and her family as new opportunities to work outside the home seemed more possible. She worked in a variety of different jobs primarily in the medical field, and later completed her graduate work in social work, becoming a social worker and psychotherapist with a cognitive-behavioral and family systems perspective.

My parents were deeply invested in my brother's and my education, and worked hard to support us both financially and emotionally in meeting our academic goals. My mother was my first academic mentor in that she spent time teaching me English, and helping me to navigate a new educational system in the U.S. My father encouraged me by telling me that my brother and I have equal intelligence. Together, my parents presented me with possibilities that had not existed for other women in our family, a gift that remains with me today and one that is unknowingly and inherently feminist.

My close relationship with my parents has not been without conflict, however. The separation from relatives and surroundings in India was deeply painful for all of us. I remember writing an essay for a newsletter of a Telegu (my first language) organization in the U.S. when I was nine years old, expressing my wish for the U.S. and India to be closer to each other in proximity. Undoubtedly, I had wished that I had choice in our move to the U.S., and that my two cultural surroundings were more similar than what was actually the case. I remember the striking contrast in physical surroundings, language, physical appearance of people, the large size of cars and buses, and the unique smells, when first arriving to the U.S. I remember disliking peanut butter sandwiches and french fries, and preferred Indian food. During our first week in school, I began to eat my food with my hands, a convention for Indian meals, instead of with utensils, and then realizing that other children were laughing at me. In later incidents at home, when someone knocked on our apartment door during our meal time, we all got up from the table and washed our hands in an attempt not to offend others. These particular memories are difficult, even now, as I realize that these incidents instigated a particular type of hiding of the self and of culture. We implicitly believed that we needed to hide how we eat, among other conventions, to survive in our new surroundings. There was no place and no one other than each other to talk with about our memories of India or our new experiences in the U.S. We did not speak openly about these experiences until my brother and I became adults. I understand the silence as reflective of the challenges involved with parents and children simultaneously negotiating new cultural space, the separation from our country of origin, and the more or less immediate need to adjust to the new culture, all of which made it difficult to articulate the depth of our personal and shared loss.

A critical component of my immigration experience concerned my wish to make sense or meaning of why we had moved, while imagining what my life would be like if we had stayed in India. Much of my internal life as a child and adolescent encompassed these ideas around culture, place, and time, as I attempted to define my identity as an Indian American girl. I found myself listening to my family and family friends in our Indian American community talk about their struggles with adjusting to the U.S., and the conflicts that existed within families, specifically those related to parent-child conflicts, marital conflict, mental illness, and violence. A growing source of conflict involved the position of women both in my family and more broadly within my Indian community while I was growing up. I grew up hearing negative comments from other Indian women about my dark skin color, an issue that permeates many Indian women's self-perceptions (Tummala-Narra, 2007). I experienced my parents as placing more restrictions in my socializing with boys, when compared with my brother. I observed the men in my family and other families assuming privileges over women, even while respecting and caring for them. Silence was a typical way of managing anxiety about inequity among men and women.

My mother's solution to these inequities for me was to encourage my independence, and secure a career path. Her encouragement contributed to my drive to move away from the domestic sphere that was mastered by my grandmothers and my mother. At the same time, the anxiety about separation from traditional caretaking roles of women in my family was evident in my experience as well as that for other women in my family and community. As I entered college, I experienced a growing desire to find meaning of my dualistic existence, one that reflected the struggle between traditional and more progressive, perhaps rebellious, conceptions of the feminine and Indian. By my third year of college, I decided to pursue a doctoral degree in clinical psychology, a field that was foreign to my family at the time.

Finding Mentors and Models

I entered graduate school in 1990, at a time when courses on multicultural psychology were not offered, and when issues of diversity were seldom addressed in courses or clinical supervision. I immersed myself in learning about Western understandings of psychopathology and healing, including cognitive-behavioral, humanistic, and psychodynamic perspectives. There were moments of critical learning that shaped my identity as a psychotherapist during this time, most poignantly in my early work with clients. As many beginning therapists, I was moved by the depth of emotional connection that was possible in this particular mode of relating. My attachments to my clients were both delightful and overwhelming. While my first experiences of clinical work involved a cognitive-behavioral orientation, my theoretical interests changed when I met my first psychoanalytic mentor, Bertram Karon, who had developed a psychoanalytic approach to working with psychotic clients. Through my supervision with Bert, I learned about the affective struggles of psychotherapists in coping with their own fear of vulnerability to major mental illness. Bert's approach was characterized by respect, honesty, genuineness, and curiosity of the therapist to better understand the client's world and his/her way of communicating particularly on the affective level. Bert would often say in supervision, "When you are in doubt of what to do [in therapy], be a human being." He also taught me the importance of diversity of theoretical thinking. He required his students to read Freud, Skinner, and Rogers as a way of understanding the depth and the breadth of psychological theories. During these early years of psychodynamic clinical training, I recognized the deepening of my connections with my clients with whom I continued to work over a number of years. In retrospect, I'm thankful for the training in working with clients in long-term psychotherapy, a possibility that is not as available to students today.

Later in graduate school, I decided to seek out my own personal psychotherapy. I chose to work with a woman, and imagined that working with a woman would allow me to feel more comfortable in sharing personal details of my life, some of which of course were unacceptable to share with my family. This experience was indeed powerful and transformative, especially considering that this was the first opportunity that I had to break my silence which had held such a strong presence in my life while growing up. Through this experience, I came to understand the therapeutic process in the more immediate sense, and the ways in which psychoanalytic psychotherapy exerts its effects in subtle, yet transformative ways.

During these early years of my clinical training, I was excited by the new theoretical ideas that I was exposed to, and yet yearned for connecting my cultural background with psychological conceptualizations of internal life. I reconnected with my Hindu spiritual heritage through studying the Bhagavad Gita, one of the primary holy books of Hinduism. I was also immersed in literature, particularly that which focused on the history of India, the struggle for independence from British rule, and poetry and essays written by the brilliant Rabindranath Tagore. I was interested in reading history from the perspective of Indians. My excitement of reading this literature was once again contained, however, as I did not have anyone at that time to talk with who could help me to synthesize my understanding of Western psychological conceptualization and Hindu spirituality and Indian philosophy. While I deeply appreciated my clinical supervisors and my therapist, I didn't know where to take this new learning. This is of course, not unusual for many ethnic minorities in clinical training. We tend to lead distinct lives separated by the personal and the professional, contributing to a "dualistic self" (Roland, 1996).

It was when I arrived to the Cambridge Hospital in Cambridge, MA as a psychology intern, and later as a post-doctoral fellow in trauma psychology, I experienced a developmental shift in addressing this silence that I have mentioned. I was also exposed to clinical supervisors and role models who struggled with issues of race, ethnicity, linguistic diversity, and socioeconomic background, all in the context of a psychodynamic approach to community based mental health care. Cambridge Hospital quickly became my professional home, as I developed strong connections with mentors such as Judith Herman and Mary Harvey at the Victims of Violence Program, who were critical sources of support as I developed my feminist and psychodynamic understandings of complex trauma. I am grateful for the women mentors in this program who offered support around my professional development beyond training, and finding balance between work and family life.

It was also during this time that my personal readings of the psychoanalytic theory, trauma psychology, multicultural psychology, and liberation psychology continued to expand such that I became increasingly interested in bridging these perspectives in my work with clients, and eventually in my scholarly writing. At this time, I had developed a series of mentors, such as Lillian Comas-Díaz, Beverly Greene, Janet Helms, and Jean Lau Chin, whom I had not met at the time. Reading their work help me to become more socially minded in my clinical practice and teaching. These psychologists value "variability and diversity of human experience" (Barrett, Chin, Comas-Díaz, Espin, Greene, & McGoldrick, 2005, p. 28), and have brought to the foreground of psychology the centrality of minority group identity and status. I felt especially hopeful when I read the works written by these brilliant women psychologists, as they found ways to bring voice to those women and ethnic and sexual minorities who had long been neglected by our field, not to mention making it possible for an Indian American psychodynamically trained psychologist to voice her ideas.

I also read the work of psychoanalysts, including Dorothy Holmes, Vamik Volkan, Salman Akhtar, Neil Altman, and Kimberlyn Leary who are scholars in the areas of immigration, race, and psychotherapy. These theorists broke new ground in psychoanalysis by attending to the long neglected areas of sociocultural context in psychoanalysis, and for me opened up the possibility for an integrative study of the inner and outer realities of my clients. Specifically, I became interested in how objective and subjective reality is constructed by the client and by the therapist, from object relations and relational psychoanalytic perspectives. Contemporary psychoanalytic theories emphasize the interaction between the subjectivity of the client and that of the therapist, and require that the therapist attend to his/her life experience as a way of better attuning to the client's internal life, and to the transference that is co-constructed by the client and the therapist (Mitchell, 1993; Stolorow, 2002). This conceptualization of the therapeutic relationship lends itself to the study of social context as it is experienced by the client and the therapist.

While the mentors that I have mentioned thus far have been pivotal to my growth as a psychologist, my clients have been at the core of my identity as a psychotherapist both in the public sector and in private practice. During and since my training, I have had the opportunity to work with clients of various cultural, religious, racial, social class, sexual identity backgrounds, and have learned some of my most valuable life lessons through these interactions. My clients have been teaching me about the unique ways in which their lives are shaped through the interaction of their personal histories and sociocultural realities. Many of my ethnic minority clients have reminded me of the difficulty of finding appropriate help and care from professionals, and of the complexity of simultaneously existing across divergent cultural contexts. Indeed I was aware of internal and external barriers to seeking help for mental health issues among the Asian Indian community, and other South Asian communities. In listening to my clients' life stories including those involving interpersonal trauma, such as sexual assault and domestic violence, and political and racial trauma, I came to understand that one of the most important functions of the psychotherapist is bearing witness to his/her clients' lives, and how bearing witness transforms the psychotherapist (Comas-Díaz, 2005). In more recent years, I have come to realize the transformative quality of making space for my clients' voices, and that when my clients have felt heard and seen (Brown, 2006), they not only feel more connected, they are better able to expand the range of life choices available to them. I've also learned to bear the seemingly paradoxical way in which I have the ability and the power to help shape my clients' lives while simultaneously feeling deeply humbled by what I feel to be my limitations as a therapist and a human being and the structural limitations within broader society that impinge on my clients' sense of freedom.

Following my post-doctoral training, I started an outpatient clinic in the department of psychiatry at the Cambridge Hospital, known at the time as the South Asian Clinic, and later as the Asian Mental Health Clinic. With the support of my clinical mentors and the administration, I directed this clinic for six years, a period of immense growth for me personally and professionally. During these years, I provided outreach to various Asian American communities on mental health issues, began developing a framework for understanding the intersection of immigration, gender, social class, and the experience of trauma, and mentored psychology, psychiatry, and social work trainees in working with individuals of Asian American background and/or ancestry. During this time at Cambridge Hospital, I initiated the first departmentwide training conferences on multicultural and psychodynamic psychotherapy. I believe that building real access to culturally competent treatment for ethnic minorities entails a responsibility that is shared by all of the clinicians in an institution, and not only those ethnic minority clinicians who primarily worked with ethnic minority clients. The chair of the Department of Psychiatry, Jack Burke, was supportive of my efforts, and I learned from him the importance of diversity being prioritized by leaders within an organization as a critical step in improving access to culturally competent care for ethnic minority clients.

This was also a period of time in which I began to write and publish my theoretical understandings of issues on immigration, trauma, and Asian American psychology. I began to find my voice, and by doing this, have been able to project the voices of my clients through my writing ever since. I was able to carry and expand these interests after moving to Washington, DC, and later to Michigan. At the Georgetown University Hospital I directed a mental health outreach program focused on trauma through the Department of Psychiatry, and at the Michigan School of Professional Psychology, I began to extend my scholarly interests in culture and immigration to the study of race and racism experienced by Asian Indians in the U.S. I wrote papers on topics such as skin color and the therapeutic relationship, immigrant mothering, and multicultural expressions of resilience among trauma survivors, integrating psychoanalytic, multicultural, and social justice perspectives. Most recently, in my academic position at Boston College, I have found ways to bring voice to concerns of ethnic minorities in ways distinct but overlapping with clinical practice. Allen Ivey (1995, 2003) suggests that psychotherapy when conceptualized as a type of liberation aims to identify individual concerns and to help the client identify ways in which their concerns are related to social context. I have found that bringing awareness of social justice issues in clinical practice, research, and teaching has been a growing emphasis in my life. I have become interested in quantitative and qualitative research focused on clinicians' perspectives on multicultural competence in psychotherapy, the experience of discrimination among first and second generation Asian Americans, and sources of resilience among survivors of trauma. I have remain engaged with scholarly writing on psychoanalytic and multicultural clinical practice emphasizing the role of race, ethnicity, and gender in the therapeutic relationship, multicultural issues in training and supervision, and the application of psychoanalytic and multicultural conceptualizations to community based programs.

Stolorow and Atwood (1979) suggest that a therapist's "pre-theoretical" values, interests, and conflicts intersect with life experiences and environment to shape his/her style of exploration and areas of emphases. Mark (1990) expands this idea of pretheoretical life of the therapist as a phenomenon that allows "a working-through and ultimately a healthful sublimation" (pp. 35-36). In considering my multicultural and psychoanalytic conceptualizations of psychotherapy, it is evident that being a psychotherapist allows for an intellectual and emotional integration of perspectives that is not typically available otherwise for me or for many of my clients. Psychoanalytic theory is centered on the analysis of conflict among opposing, contradictory, and sometimes unacceptable feelings and thoughts, and embedded in its core is an emphasis on introspection and subjective experience. It seems to make sense then that I would be drawn to a theory that addresses internal conflict as imposed by external situations and demands. This particular lens has allowed me to better understand my own conflicts related to identity in the face of cultural upheaval and change, and to better empathize with my clients who face parallel conflicts. Multicultural psychology provides a lens for integrating social, political, and cultural realities into the understanding of individual and interpersonal conflicts. At the present time, I am immersed in building dialogue across theoretical perspectives, and across difference more broadly. I am mindful of those times when voice and dialogue have been absent in my life, and recognize that this is when I have felt a cost to my sense of identity. I believe that this is the experience of many people who are at the margins of society in one sense or another.

Facing Race

Experiences of racism directed against ethnic minority psychotherapists by clients, students, supervisors, and colleagues have been documented in recent years (Ali, Flojo, Chronister, Hayashino, Smiling, Torres, & McWhirter, 2005; Rastogi & Woolford-Hunt, 2005). As a graduate student, I had an experience when a fellow student, a White woman, commented to me after a group supervision session about how surprised she was that I was so assertive in a session with my client when I had confronted him about a difficult exchange that I had with him the previous week. When I asked her why she was surprised, she told me that she did not expect this from an Indian woman. At the moment, I was both stunned and angry, and felt unable to articulate a clear response to her. She had already decided who I was as an Indian woman without asking any questions or learning anything about my background. In my experience, Indian women were not passive, as she had implied, but rather were powerful in many ways. However, this was not the dominant narrative.

Over the past five years, I've revisited my earlier interests in the dynamics of race and racial discrimination. Specifically, I've been interested in experiences of racial discrimination and trauma among Asian Indians and more broadly, immigrant communities. I have found the study of race in literary works written by Chinua Achebe, Homi Bhaba, and Salman Rushdie of particular interest. These writers challenge post-colonial conceptions of the "third world." They challenge us to consider indigenous narratives spoken and written by individuals who are native to a particular country or community. This idea of indigenous narrative is most relevant to psychotherapy, as we seek to hear the voice of the client from his/her perspective, even though his/her voice may not be heard and may be distorted by those who possess more power in broader social, cultural, or political contexts. These literary works remind us that as psychotherapists, we are in a position to help our clients write their versions of history, rather than those imposed by others. In doing so, over time, I have experienced myself more authentically as a psychotherapist, and more generally as a human being. I am now better able to talk about my own background and inquire about that of others, when interacting with my clients, students, and colleagues, in a way that engages and encourages dialogue rather than perpetuating misconceptions and emotional distance.

Over the past several years, I've become involved with the American Psychological Association (APA), specifically as the chair of the Multicultural Concerns Committee of the APA Division of Psychoanalysis (Div. 39), and member of the APA Committee on Ethnic Minority Affairs (CEMA). I am grateful to my mentor, Jaine Darwin and past president of Division 39, David Ramirez for suggesting that I become involved with Div. 39 at a time when I was unsure about what it would be like for an Indian woman to be a member of the division of psychoanalysis, despite my deep interest in psychoanalytic ideas. Taking these risks has been essential to my learning. I have found that becoming involved within Division 39 and CEMA has offered spaces for increased dialogue with colleagues on issues of racial and cultural diversity, and the possibility of shifting these issues to the foreground of psychology, as there continues to be a tendency for these issues to be marginalized in the field of psychology. My work as a psychotherapist has also been enriched through my experiences with APA, as I have learned more about the ways in which policy and sociopolitical awareness can promote positive and effective change in my clients' lives.

Becoming a Mother and Being a Female Psychotherapist

In a recent article published in *American Psychologist*, Cheung and Halpern (2010) highlight the fact that a double standard regarding the presence of children is "alive and well in the workplace" (p. 183), in which men who have children are typically thought to have stability, whereas the opposite is true for women. These realities point to a conflict with which many female psychotherapists struggle. However, the issue of mothering and its impact on the professional lives of women has not been adequately addressed in the psychological literature.

Some of the most transformative times of my life as a psychotherapist involved my pregnancies and the birth of my two sons. Pregnancy presents conflicts between the needs of clients and the therapist's own needs (Notman & Nadelson, 2004). Indeed, for me, these changes involved tremendous physical and psychological change. As with other developmental shifts, such as involvement in a romantic relationship or marriage, I felt a deep sense of joy and preoccupation with the anticipation of new beginnings. With some of my clients, I felt as though the caretaking roles had somehow reversed, when they asked how I was feeling or if I had morning sickness. Other clients wondered if I would leave them, and worried that I no longer needed them in my life, and that the baby would replace them. The confluence of maternal transference and countertransference was at times overwhelming, and yet at the same time presented opportunities for deeper therapeutic work. These were the moments when my clients could more immediately access their feelings about their parents, children, and other significant others, about their feelings about me as their therapist, and their particular life struggles.

Becoming a mother in many ways shifted what it meant to be a psychotherapist. I was better able to identify resiliency of parents and children, and to empathize with the challenges of parenting under stressful circumstances. I came to live the realities of balancing work and family life, something that remains largely invisible to mainstream society, even while many mothers do not have access to adequate help and resources. Caretaking both in the family and with clients becomes a task that is both fulfilling and challenging, one that requires ongoing negotiation throughout one's life. I believe that mothering, as with other important developmental shifts, transforms the inner and outer life of a female psychotherapist. For example, I routinely tell new clients that I will keep my cell phone on vibrate mode, as I need to answer the phone if the call concerns my children. This is a necessary reality, as my husband's work does not permit him to respond to phone calls during most hours in the day. In the sense of internal change, I sometimes find myself thinking of my children and their safety when a client discusses painful traumatic material.

These shifts are important to note, in that they are often particular to the experience of women. They further remind us of the importance of self-care and support. It is not uncommon for women to experience their real life struggles as indications of poor performance or incompetence, amidst seeking balance between work and family. In some cases, women may find themselves engaged with what Lynne Layton (2004) has termed, "defensive autonomy," where those attributes linked with maternal or relational are denigrated as a way of coping with intimacy needs. Mothers who are psychotherapists are at a risk for denying or minimizing the need for support and care, as they are in many ways required to be caretakers. For many ethnic minority women, mothering further entails the negotiation of cultural change, extended family, and revisiting acculturative processes and spirituality (Tummala-Narra, 2004, 2009).

Since becoming a mother, I have developed an appreciation for my husband, parents, other family members, friends, and colleagues who have supported me in finding ways to manage the physical and psychological demands of parenting. My mentors have become friends over the years, and this has been an important source of strength in facing challenges of parenting, relocations and transitions, and navigating difficult moments in work with clients. Another source of strength has been my connection with my Hindu spiritual faith and Indian cultural heritage, which has transformed my life as a parent as I work to pass on our spiritual and cultural values to our children. Over the past several years, I've been able to talk more with my family, friends, and colleagues about the ways that I integrate my spiritual life, cultural background, and my theoretical (psychoanalytic and multicultural) ideas, bringing together previously disparate parts of my life. I believe that my own ability to bring the various aspects of my personal, professional, and multicultural experiences together in these interactions has been changing the way that I interact with clients, possibly in a way that facilitates their ability to bear and negotiate multiple social and cultural realities.

Concluding Comments: Lessons Learned

I will conclude by summing up a few lessons that may be helpful to women psychotherapists, and to those women who are training to become psychotherapists. First, the awareness of one's own personal history and its influence on one's life is critical to understanding one's interests and goals as a psychotherapist. Becoming and being aware of one's subjectivity helps the therapist engage with the client's subjective experience with more depth and clarity. This type of awareness is also important in helping the therapist cope with difficult life transitions, separations, and losses. The endeavor of knowing oneself further entails attention to social, political, and cultural histories and realities.

Second, women psychotherapists have unique challenges with social expectations and demands related to their gender roles and to power in their relationships with men and other women. Having female and male mentors who recognize our ability to define our female identity as professionals and women on our own terms, our strength and resiliency are one of the most valuable gifts that we can receive and pass on to students whom we supervise and teach. The relational psychoanalyst Adrienne Harris (2002) has pointed out the ways in which female agency continues to be tied with men's positions of power, both through actual interactions between men and women, and through unconscious identifications. Having the mentorship of women, such as my mother and several women psychologists, has been critical to my growth as a psychotherapist, partly because the women who mentored me communicated to me that I was capable of creating my own unique voice as a therapist and leader. I take the issue of mentoring my students seriously at least in part because I know the value of strong mentoring in my life.

Finally, being involved in the world outside of psychotherapy informs our understanding of the internal and external realities of clients, and can help us offer expanded knowledge and skills in our work with clients. My intellectual and emotional growth as a therapist has not only been shaped through training and ongoing supervision and consultation, but through engaging with diverse literature and diverse communities, and learning about different understandings of emotional distress and approaches to healing. This type of experiencing is among the most enjoyable and fulfilling as I continue to learn more about difference and commonality across cultural contexts. In retrospect, I must have felt like a psychologist or healer in some way as a child, negotiating multiple transitions amidst cultural change in a more or less isolated process, despite having a loving family. However, becoming a psychotherapist has involved layers of introspection, risk taking, finding voice, and making space for voice, all of which was possible through connecting with remarkable people in my life. In this way, I believe that I am at home as a psychotherapist as the narratives rooted in different parts of my life coexist even as they pose conflict and possibility.

References

Ali, S. R., Flojo, J. R., Chronister, K. M., Hayashino, D., Smiling, Q. R., Torres, D., & McWhirter, E. H. (2005). When racism is reversed: Therapists of color speak about their experiences with racism from clients, supervisees, and supervisors. In M. Rastogi & E. Wieling (Eds.), *Voices of color: First-person accounts of ethnic minority therapists*, pp. 117-133. Thousand Oaks, CA: Sage.

Barrett, S. E., Chin, J. L., Comas-Díaz, L., Espin, O., Greene, B., & McGoldrick, M. (2005). Multicultural feminist therapy: Theory in context. *Women & Therapy, 28*, 27-61.

Brown, L. S. (2006). Still subversive after all these years: The relevance of feminist therapy in the age of evidence-based practice. *Psychology of Women Quarterly, 30*, 15-24.

Cantor, D. W. (1990). Women as therapists: What we already know. In D. W. Cantor (Ed.), *Women as therapists*, pp. 3-19. Northvale, NJ: Jason Aronson.

Cheung, F. M., & Halpern, D. F. (2010). Women at the top: Powerful leaders define success as work + family in a culture of gender. *American Psychologist, 65*(3), 182-193.

Comas-Díaz, L. (2005). Becoming a multicultural psychotherapist: The confluence of culture, ethnicity, and gender. *Journal of Clinical Psychology, 61*(8), 973-981.

Harris, A. (2002). Mothers, monsters, mentors. *Studies in Gender and Sexuality, 3*(3), 281-295.

Ivey, A. E. (1995). Psychotherapy as liberation: Toward specific skills and strategies in multicultural counseling and therapy. In J. Ponterotto, J. Casas, L. Suzuki, & C. Alexander (Eds.), *Handbook of multicultural counseling*, pp. 53-72. Thousand Oaks, CA: Sage.

Ivey, A. E., & Collins, N. M. (2003). Social justice: A long-term challenge for counseling psychology. *The Counseling Psychologist, 31*(3), 290-298.

Layton, L. (2004). Working nine to nine: The new women of prime time. *Studies in Gender and Sexuality, 5*(3), 351-369.

Mark, C. B. (1990). The personal relationship between therapists and their theoretical orientation. In D. W. Cantor (Ed.), *Women as therapists*, pp. 33-54. Northvale, NJ: Jason Aronson.

Mitchell, S. A. (1993). *Hope and dread in psychoanalysis*. New York: Basic Books.

Notman, M. T., & Nadelson, C. C. (2004). Gender in the consulting room. *Journal of the American Academy of Psychoanalysis and Dynamic Psychiatry, 32*(1), 193-200.

Rastogi, M., & Woolford-Hunt, C. (2005). International academic sojourners in the United States of America: Color in the Ivory tower. In M. Rastogi & E. Wieling (Eds.), *Voices of color: First-person accounts of ethnic minority therapists*, pp. 211-229. Thousand Oaks, CA: Sage.

Roland, A. (1996). *Cultural pluralism and psychoanalysis: The Asian and North American experience*. New York: Routledge.

Stolorow, R. D. (2002). From drive to affectivity: Contextualizing psychological life. *Psychoanalytic Inquiry, 22,* 678–685.

Stolorow, R. D., & Atwood, G. E. (1979). *Faces in a cloud, subjectivity in personality theory*. New York: Jason Aronson.

Tummala-Narra, P. (2004). Mothering in a foreign land. *American Journal of Psychoanalysis, 64*(2), 165-180.

Tummala-Narra, P. (2007). Skin color and the therapeutic relationship. *Psychoanalytic Psychology, 24*(2), 255-270.

Tummala-Narra, P. (2009). Contemporary impingements on mothering. *American Journal of Psychoanalysis, 69,* 4-21.

Unbroken Chain

10

CARLA BRADSHAW

THIS IS WHAT I THINK. On close examination we are each a contradiction in terms, living inherent paradoxes proclaiming this and yet doing that. We are who we say we are, and we are not. This is not a criticism, it is just the way we try on and change ourselves over time. The particulars of this odyssey are the stuff of our individualism.

Social justice and social privilege, the Grateful Dead and Motown, national and internationalism, poverty and privilege, color and not color, are the stuff of my own character. Some of these things are hard to reveal. Not for shame, at least not anymore, but because of the privacy within which I have treasured and nurtured this understanding.

This is part of a story. It is about a journey. It is a story about journeys as well . . . paths taken and off-road meanderings that have at times been more important than the planned journey ever was. This is a story about the importance of planning, so that there is a path, and the even greater importance of taking opportunities when they occur. This is the gist of what I would advise. *Take the leap. Refuse to be broken. Have friends who are not therapists. Have friends who are. Healing the world, even just one person, is doing a lot. Pass it on.*

When does the journey of our lives begin? Does it start at that moment when one decides the course of one's life? Or, does it begin long before birth, like a destiny or fate? How is the journey molded and altered by the whimsy of unforeseen events that make up the school of hard knocks? No one makes the journey alone, really. Much of mine was molded by people both known and unknown to me. I say this because I know that just as I have tried to help people behind the scenes, there have been generous, kind people who have worked for me anonymously. It wouldn't be true or fair to fail to acknowledge this.

Aside from this, all of what I have come to know as my journey has been wrought by the alchemical influence of those who have both loved me and hated me. My struggle with both shaped and defined me. It would be difficult to say that those who loved me exerted a larger effect than those who hated me. I could only say that I couldn't have thrived without them. As for the other, given my choice, I would have done without them, but to have done so, I probably wouldn't be me today. So, looking back, I would have to say thank you to both. Having thrived, this is possible to say.

Luck also has a lot to do it. For without either luck or the ability to recognize a lucky situation and seize it, there is no telling the opportunities that would have been missed. These lucky points in my life were gifts, often unearned (that's what makes it luck), that propelled or verified that I was on track. Overall, looking back, it is probably the appearance of these lucky moments that has always signaled to me that I was still on my correct path.

To be sure, there have been times when I mistook temptation, in the Faustean sense, for luck. These haven't been nice times. In my life, perhaps in yours as well, the truly lucky moments were often like jet streams, a sudden propulsion into a new vector . . . of opportunity, satisfaction and even happiness. Even riding the jet stream is sometimes hard and painful . . . causing doubt. Looking back, I think I felt the difference between a hard time that resulted from a wrong turn, and a hard time that wrought improvement. Even though I think that the ability to leap on opportunity is learned over time, as is the ability to discern false from true opportunities, I also think that emboldened by the net of those who believe in us and encourage us, aiming true with the aid of their good advice, we learn that we can leap and risk at those unplanned moments when things happen just because you happened to be on that path. No one does it alone.

Becoming a Woman Psychotherapist

I began growing up in the late 1950s in what must have been postwar Japan on the upswing. There was no hot running water and no municipal sewer system where I lived. In fact, there were no foreigners that I knew of. I had been there since such a young age that I thought I was native and that my father was the foreigner. So, I called him "gai-jin." I was pampered, carried, carefree, and doted upon especially by my grandmother who was magical, solid, and soft. She showed up when I was afraid and gave me dreams about white snakes with green eyes. She made me feel as though I was destined to be in this life. I didn't feel different, even while knowing that I was, because my father was "America-jin," and I felt special.

First grade in San Francisco, second grade in Seattle, third and fourth grades in Yokohama, fifth grade on in Chicago. I felt different and maybe was different from this time on. The feeling of specialness changed. I grew up on *Rear Window*, *Through a Glass Darkly*, *Roshomon*, *The Seven Samurai*, *The Cabinet of Dr. Caligari*, *Psycho*, *Suddenly Last Summer*, *The Birds*, and *The Three Faces of Eve*. Psychological autopsy was dinnertime conversation and emotional dissection of other people's motives was common. We had what seemed an inherent interest in what drove other people and ourselves. It was a long time before I could see that hidden silently beneath the conversation and closeness, driven by the traumas of my parents' early lives, we trusted very few, maybe no one. We were different almost everywhere we went and we compensated by trying at being better than. Better or worse, we felt insecure. It all seemed natural. It was a Freudian world of firstborns and only children until my brothers came along.

How many of us spent our early years, maybe pre-adolescent years onward being the listening ear for our friends, parents, and other family members? I suspect a number of us, who become psychotherapists later, may have begun this way. I cannot imagine how else the concept of the "parentified child" would have become so well accepted by therapists everywhere. Most psychotherapists recognize the feeling from their own lives, I suspect. I certainly did. It was an experience of contrasting forces . . . at times basking in the privileges of being a confidant which sometimes bred feelings of disloyalty, burdened and brimming with secrets, feeling like a true or best friend only to have some move on as soon as the crisis of the moment had passed, becoming skilled at the art of one-way conversations in which the other does most of the talking and revealing. I learned to listen and to stay hidden. How odd to feel so alone and yet so inside the world of others. It was one way to have a place. It was a long time later that I realized this: the careful positioning at the periphery of gatherings and interactions is a survival strategy when you are not feeling like other people. In my case, it would be a long time before I felt like other people.

I am embarrassed to admit it, but I was a very heterosexual girl. I am not sure that I gave any thought to same sex relationships until I entered college. The myopia of this, looking back, is hard to believe of myself and reminds me what a privilege it is to be conventional, as unconventional as I felt. This is particularly poignant to me because my high school boyfriend turned out to be a gay man, as was my best male friend in high school. I chose and was chosen by gay teenagers to be close. I didn't know it then, and I don't think they did either that we might have recognized in each other that outlier feeling that we felt in common. None of this was known to me at the time, not their gay identity nor my affinity for outliers.

I know that in my late college years when one is required to declare what we will be doing with our lives, it felt like a guilty secret to look for a career that would balance with my unexamined notions of having a husband and children. It wasn't that I aspired to these last two things, I just never thought anything else. The sense that I was being shallow bothered me, but I couldn't move constructively beyond this sense. It just hung there until serendipity changed me.

In the summer of my junior year in college, a professor in sociology urged me to take summer quarter in San Francisco as part of a program she and her husband, also a professor, sponsored. We would get academic credits, I could graduate early, and pad my transcript even more! It was 1977. I had been working with her coding newspaper articles for references to violence against women. Combing the back pages of local newspapers for words: "rape," "assault," "domestic violence," and such. It started as padding for my college transcript, but it ended in my lifelong dedication to feminism. The Haight Ashbury thing was already 10 years past and I was sorry I missed it. What I hadn't missed was left politics. For a girl at a Midwestern college, the allure of California was irresistible... the warmth, the sun, the ocean. I was still a straight girl. The chance to go West under the guise of scholarship would stop my parents' objections cold. What could be better? I found an apartment in the Castro District of San Francisco, couldn't understand why the beautiful men had no interest in me, and began working as staff intern at La Casa de Las Madres, I was told, the first battered women's shelter in the United States. I woke up. It was also the years of Jill Johnston's "Lesbian Nation." I lived where Harvey Milk worked and was killed. I woke up, some more.

San Francisco was where, years before, my Chinese friend and I were spanked nearly every day by the purple haired lady in front of our first grade class. We didn't know why. It didn't hurt when she bent first one of us, then the other over her lap and hit our bottoms. But we both burned with embarrassment standing in front of the class. We didn't know why. I could only figure many years later that it was because we were Japanese and Chinese. I cannot remember any other differences to make sense of the experience. I was only there a school year because my father was a lawyer. My friend, he may have never left there, because his family was large and poor. I often wonder what happened to him. I felt glad to have gotten away and disloyal. To him.

To be fair, I was very special in second grade, in the Northwest, and special still at the beginning of third grade in Iowa. What had been an inexplicable source of punishment turned into a source of unearned esteem and credibility. Specialness. By then, I knew that ethnicity and notions of race were involved. My value in these new locales on the basis of the status my race/ethnicity conferred, because I was different, for reasons that were not obvious to me, came at a formative time so that the oddly elevated experience in second and third grades helped me every bit as much as my first grade experience had hurt me. The odd realization even at a young age was that I had been devalued and elevated, and that it was not really about me.

One last experience formed an important part of me. In fourth grade I loved and was in love with my best friend who was Black. To be mixed in Japan was odd and at times hard. To be mixed and Black in Japan was very lonely. He and I understood this and we clung to each other. Love in fourth grade can't last, and it isn't forgotten either.

Somewhere in the midst of growing up, my family broke. We stayed together, but we broke. The breakage threw shards in all directions so that we all could feel the wreckage, even though it was invisible, and the wounds bled unseen. We each wore our wound differently, in very personal ways. No one went unscathed. My mother bore the worst of it, and was responsible most for how it turned out. None of the psychological autopsies nor the conjecture about the motivations of others kept us safe from ourselves. The pressures on our multiracial, multiethnic, masquerading-as-though-we-didn't-notice family couldn't be kept out. That is what I think now, but I have never asked them what they may think. It would be a very long time before the breakage healed. It did heal though, and that, it turns out, is most important.

I became a woman therapist because that is what I was fated to be. I was smart, I was diligent, and my family loved me with all their brokenness. I had privilege to escape adversity, and this in turn allowed me to reexamine the events from a safer distance. This allowed me to understand what had been my fault, and what had been perpetrated on me. Without such distance, I may have decided that it had all been personal. I know that many who have suffered racism and misogyny do not have this option. Had I not become a psychologist, would I have understood the many layers of meaning these experiences held? On top of all of this, I had access to opportunities that set me up. It was the early years of feminism. I benefited from Title 9, but not as much as it benefits girls today. I am happy about that. It was the middle years of the civil rights movement, and I benefited from that as well. My roles in life had paved a course that made psychology as natural in some ways as speaking. Speaking out was still hard.

The feelings of being "other" were supported by experiences of being discriminated against so that I learned that intolerance is real, often subtle, but also often unabashed and still there were times when no one would stand up (even me). I also knew that some of these feelings of alienation were self-indulgent and self-pitying. The current of national events supported my desires, and key people helped to make it happen. I am also a woman therapist because I had lived with the persistent experience of alienation, but I was privileged, so that I had places to turn for refuge or simply to escape. Access, resources, and education. Having these (I did know even then what a privilege this was) gave me the opportunity to do what I probably do best. I was lucky to have been shown the pain in the lives of women in the uneven power balance of unquestioned patriarchy so that I could recognize it, the struggle for acceptance and freedom that was the gay movement in 1977 in San Francisco, and these along with my personal experiences made becoming a Ph.D. part of riding the large current of social change, part of my own personal expression and experiment. Because people recognized and helped me, I was able to do it. I really have never looked back nor regretted it. It was a correct decision.

Being a Female Psychotherapist

I think the majority of psychotherapists in the United States today are female. The membership of the American Psychological Association is 55.7% women (APA, 2009). It was not so when I was in training. It was still a man's world in psychology, and I think in the world of practicing psychotherapists. Yet the changes that are now obvious were apparent then; that women would be entering the field in large numbers because the intersection of access to advanced credentials and interest in a helping profession is probably a natural fit. Even though these are the current demographics, there is a persistent feeling that much of our fundamentals are still grounded in men's experience, thereby under-representing and misunderstanding the important differences in the experiences of women and girls. For women in academia, the glass ceiling of wage and promotion differentials is real. Compounding this difficulty is the complexity inherent in extrapolating to the experiences of men or women of color as well as the experiences of GBTQ (gay, bisexual, trans-sexual, queer) men and women. Adding the experiences of the differently able, whether born with or acquired, adds yet more layers of necessary awareness that is integral to the lens of fairness, balance, and perspective. It is a compulsory yet mind-numbing task to pay serious attention to the various ways in which a person's identity and communities of belonging are essential to understanding anyone. One never knows the true story of a person until an artful exchange of questions and stories has revealed the myriad of personal identities that they hold dear and abhor. There is probably no substitution for the truth that emerges out of the details of our many thought ways and lifeways (I owe this phrase to Joseph Trimble, 2007). In our professional jargon, this is now referenced as intersecting identities.

So, regarding my thought ways and lifeways as a female psychotherapist, I am a woman, a person of color at a time in the United States when my color may no longer be a color, a psychologist, a massage therapist/body worker on the side, wife, mother, lover of gardens and animals, a Jew by choice, a Buddhist and atheist by birth, a believer of the spiritual and spirits, and an avid observer of things. I wish I was an artist, a social activist, and able to leap tall obstacles in a single bound. Staying true to feminist notions of attention to inherent power hierarchies in therapy, weaving social consciousness and social justice into how therapy is transacted, attending carefully to gender interactions as well as the multiple levels of many –isms: ablism, lookism (because phenotype and notions of beauty as well as ugly create real disparities), racism, classism, empiricism (because not all that is true can be measured), sometimes feels like leaping obstacles of many sizes that are strewn all over the place. It is hard to do it well consistently. However, it really is a perpetual process in the sense that none of us actually gets finally free of perpetrating these -isms. It is really important to keep trying and to keep open to confrontation.

Gendered Experiences

Being pregnant. This is perhaps the quintessential gendered event in a woman psychotherapist's experience. It is an unavoidably intrusive event in the therapy that reveals private facts about the female therapist's life. Being pregnant advertises that you have had sex, at least once, if you are heterosexual. I imagine that it brings up even more complicated, intimate questions if you are lesbian, at least among heterosexual clients. I was lucky to have had clients at the time who were willing to speak up and talk about their musings and wonderings. People did talk about their joys with and about children, but more often, they talked about their losses, regrets, and wishes. For some women, my pregnancies brought up their wishes for a child, or lost children, or regrets about children, but the women rarely talked about the sex part. For men, some of the longing for children arose, but as a heterosexual woman, so did fantasies about sex with me. For some male clients the idea arose because it was obvious that I had had sex, at least once or twice. For others, sexual fantasies dissipated because it was obvious that I am sexual with someone else in my life. In a few situations, a difference between the pregnant me and the client emerged that had not been there before; some people don't like or want children and wondered whether I thought that was okay. For the gay and lesbian clients at the time, the longing for parity in society about children and relationships emerged. This is when I first heard the term "breeder." So, there was hostility too. It seems as though the culture of the Northwest today is much more accepting of those in gay and lesbian relationships having children, but marriage disparity persists.

Though there isn't adequate space to speak fully about the clinical issues related to the pregnant therapist, I would offer a short list of important other client concerns. Clients variously worried about whether I would really return to my practice, whether I would still see them, felt angry about the inconveniences to them, worried and resented the time off of therapy necessitated by my maternity leave, and some struggled with the necessity to consider whether they were best served by transferring to another therapist. Transferring to another practitioner was in some cases a very good experience and for others, more fretful. Having good therapist friends available for referral was invaluable. For some, the loss of their notions of specialness to me was troublesome and required very delicate dialogue. Still others worried about the fate of the unborn child whether it would survive gestation, birth, even childhood.

If that is a short list of what clients expressed, here is a short list of what I felt. I felt elated to be pregnant and eager to meet my child. I was worried about the welfare of the clients feeling at times guilty, disloyal, tired, myself fretful, and at times avoidant of difficult conversations that I knew were going to happen. One word of reassurance—each time I left my private practice, each time for about 10 months, I was able to return to many former clients who were willing to return as well. Each time my practice rebuilt. Even though we face more uncertain economic as well as health care policy environments than in the late 1980s and early 1990s, my sense from supervisees is that this is still generally true when maternity leave interrupts an established practice. Again, there is so much more to say here, since there are many variables that may exert various effects. In my case, this was how it went.

Pregnancy opened a door into seeking facts about me that would ordinarily be inhibited by the power structure of therapy, probably because my stretching body shape was undeniable and gave tacit permission to stretch unspoken presumed boundaries. This is one instance in which feminism was so helpful. As an early career trainee in psychoanalysis and psychodynamic psychotherapy, the proscriptions against too much self-disclosure would have been very hard. As it was, derivative self-disclosure was inevitable and unavoidable! So, I engaged in conversations about sex, longing, sexual orientation, social roles, privilege, absence, and loss in ways that I would not have conceived in my limited experience at the time. This probably shifted my psychodynamic tendencies toward non-disclosure forever in the direction of evaluating a psychotherapy client's right to know about me. There really needs to be more literature about pregnancy and the female therapist.

Being a mother. So much of child raising is about restraint and expansion. On the restraint side, there was a lot I could not do because I was committed to raising my children in a way that we as a family would all know that we were there for each other. It seemed as though there were many professional opportunities that were foregone or forfeited because of my needs to do what I thought was a good job. Still, I overcommitted at times, underperformed at times, and felt really stretched as well. In the middle years of child raising that are spent in a support role on the sides of soccer fields, or next to the bathtub, or in front of the stove, or quietly in a dark room waiting to tiptoe out without getting called back, I often wondered or narcissistically lamented what I could have done, or might have become professionally in the "woulda, coulda" sort of way. In those years when so much of me seemed subsumed in the needs of babies and children, I would give in to lamentations about missed chances, roads not taken. But here is an instance in which I was lucky. I had daughters who raised me because we matched each other in temperament and they talked to me all along the way. Through them I met friends I wouldn't have known otherwise because the parents of our children's friends become our community as well. These communities allowed me to see what people think about, how they think, and what other people's lives are like who are not psychotherapists. Learning about people through our role as psychotherapists doesn't give the same perspective as just being another one in a group. Granted my children grew up, but I was raised up. This was a great expansion.

Two sources of tremendous support not only got me through these years, but helped me sustain a vibrant participation in psychology as well. The husband, whom the young heterosexual girl really did marry and have children with, is also a feminist man. I don't know that he would say this about himself, but he is. He has never wavered about the fact that I still have the name I was given at birth and that was only a shred of the individual identity I demanded over time. From their birth, he was and is as interested in being with our daughters as I. He experienced the restraints and expansions, both personal and professional, just as I did. I was able to leave our babies with him to write, to maintain a business, to keep a toe in professional activities and to keep my friends. His gift to me of his natural love for his daughters is beyond any measure. For me, that he is this way is pure luck. I know I didn't have the acumen to have known this about his character 10 years earlier. He has shown it to me over time. He understands that I don't need much, except the huge thing of knowing that there is one person in my life who really loves me. This is quite a burden that I wouldn't put on my children but I want my partner to accept.

My women psychologist friends were the other stalwarts in my life. They were there to say "change the locks" when I was in a bad relationship, they were there to say " you can do this" when I was so tired, so feeling small, or so feeling inadequate that I wanted to stop whatever important thing to me that I was attempting. They said to me, "don't shrink, don't act so meekly" in paraphrase when my self-confidence had left me and I was in a professional situation in which I felt like an imposter. They knew that I wasn't. They were also there when my ability to be a better friend took a backseat to being a parent. When as a parent I needed advice and help, they gave it with love and expertise that didn't hold back. Without these women, I wouldn't be writing right now. I didn't really earn their friendship because they gave it so freely. I feel sure that my life wouldn't have the joy in it that it does without these friends. I pay it back and pass it on.

The Female Healing Experience

We can make our minds so like still water
that beings gather about us
that they may see,
it may be,
their own images,
and so live for a moment

with a clearer, perhaps even with a fiercer life
because of our quiet.
—W.B. Yeats (1893, 1902), *Celtic Twilight*

Now in my 27th year of private practice, I still grapple with the essential questions about psychotherapy:

- What are the active ingredients for inducing (influencing, persuading, encouraging) change in people that lasts? Although psychotherapy outcome research has yet to be definitive about this, much of this research still yields to the therapeutic alliance as the most potent factor. However, the therapist's therapeutic orientation affects how the therapist will select and organize the information clients provide. This in turn may even affect whether and how the therapeutic alliance is used. The interaction between these two important factors, orientation and alliance, can be understood, at least by the individual therapist, even though it would be very complex to tease this out in research designs. In this way we could each seek to understand our most effective traits as therapists.
- What are the therapist's factors that best influence this alliance? Is it primarily a matter of the well-worn psychotherapy notions such as safety, understanding, and empathy? Or, could it be that these are necessary but also merely the beginnings of a more potent collaborative alliance? If so, what are the attributes of an even more robust collaboration?
- What is the nature of human nature?
- Can psychotherapy remain separate from spirituality, and if it can, should it?

Psychotherapy research offers some guidance in addressing these questions; however, we each seek and find our own resolutions. In my mind, this is the most exhilarating aspect of the professional journey. Studying the nature of human nature initiates a meandering, fascinating exploration of many areas of knowledge that today should include sciences outside of psychology, such as biology, anthropology, sociology, physiology, neurosciences, organ and body systems, pharmacology, philosophy, metaphysics, and physics. I also think that the psychotherapist gains a great deal from the study of mythology, fiction, religious, and spiritual works, all of which directly speak to the nature of human nature. It appears to me that we are emerging from an era of deep specialization in the fields of health care, and we seem to be moving toward a convergence as our sophisticated technologies point toward integration. We see this, for example, as the neurosciences are now illuminating the brain bases of interpersonal interactions (Cozolino, 2002). This in turn points again to the evolutionary, biological importance of relating to other people. My own dabbling into these various fields yielded the conclusion consistent with people such as Maturana and Varela (1991), Maddock and Larson (1995), Teilhard de Chardin (1959), that: all systems seek increasing complexity and as a part of this imperative, humans seek movement always toward "becoming." So, for me, I have concluded that at its most elemental, psychotherapy offers companionship to clients seeking their better selves. While I don't think clients see this necessarily at the onset of therapy, I do think that this aspect must be engaged and the collaboration on this goal established for the therapeutic change to matter enough to hold.

This view of the personal evolution of a "better self" is not judgmental. It acknowledges the lifelong nature of maturing. We know it as the process of "becoming." Psychotherapy at its best urges the process toward personal improvement and systemic improvement; i.e., the good of the part and the whole. It seems to me that viewed in this way, whether the modality of therapy is primarily behavioral, cognitive, emotional, interpersonal, intrapersonal, or systemic; the kind of change that lasts occurs when one's view of one's own world, past and present, shifts; that is, it doesn't look the same anymore. The word "world" as used here refers to the sense we each have of our experiences, the people who comprise our family, communities, cultures, and nations of origin and residence. In other words, the whole of the internal psychological context within which we place ourselves. As in a paradigm shift, the change is structural. Literally, the premises upon which former conclusions were built are changed. When this happens in psychotherapy, not only does the world not look the same, one doesn't look the same to oneself anymore either. So, the shift seems to occur on all the levels listed even though the mode of access (therapeutic orientation) may have been primarily via one modality (cognitive, emotional, interpersonal, intrapersonal, systemic, etc.). When the meaning of events and behaviors in our lives change, our physiology relative to these events changes as well, and our sense of our own place in the world (past and present) also shifts. It is psychotherapy when these all happen for the better.

One of the hardest transitions for me as a female psychotherapist has been to support myself in being less nice. There is so much niceness expected out of women and also psychotherapists. Whether it is to be nice to other women, or to men, or just to everybody, as an extension of the stereotype of women, this is the expectation. I don't mean that I am not nice. I mean that I don't lead from a position of niceness to signal the "safety" of psychotherapy with me. I don't emphasize being understanding either, for the same reason. I don't want to be a safe person or to create this kind of safe place (Schnarch, 1991) for people. (Much of my thinking regarding notions of seeking one's better self, safety in psychotherapy, being known, and being willing to know are owing to the work of David Schnarch who integrates these ideas deeply into his trainings in the *Crucible* approach.)

I know that this is a kind of sacrilege. Especially under conditions of knowing the abject lack of safety some women and girls experience, and that people of color experience, and that all kinds of people experience, shouldn't I offer safety? I can't. That is what I conclude. It is not that I don't want to. It is more that I can't because, in my mind, we have something much better to offer. We offer a paradigm shift. It is in the nature of psychotherapy to potentiate change in the person identified as "client." This is inherently "dangerous" because such change always ventures into unknown territory. Yet, this is what those who become "clients" seek. With regard to understanding, we offer what we can within the range of our tolerance, expertise, intellect, empathy, and feeling. But is this "safe"? Referring back to how I began this discourse, who among us is not a living contradiction? Who really wants to be understood? *It is one thing to want to be understood for what we want to be understood as. It is really something else to be seen and understood as we are.* This is much less fun and to engage such a process is at its very core an act of courage and trust. What it is not is "safe." (Recall that this is coming from one whose emotional origins involved honing the presentation of the "as if" from the perimeters of interpersonal engagement.)

In this sense, when we undertake a role as psychotherapist, we are offering companionship on an intimate journey that may be harrowing for all participants. We are as likely to be changed by the client as they by us. It is a reciprocal process that we as therapists tend to talk about mostly uni-directionally. However, it is part of the collaboration that we as therapists tend not to openly acknowledge, but must accept. While it may be true that approaches differ on various dimensions, I don't think any of them work without this contract having been made; that we agree to collaborate on an exploration that is mostly uni-directional. The therapists offer the best of what they have at the time: empathy, expertise, tolerance, understanding, and a commitment to bringing about change in someone else's life, and to take the problems that arise in our own, whether it is caused by the therapy we offer or by something else, somewhere else to solve.

How problems for therapists can arise external to the therapy is probably easy to imagine. How can doing therapy cause problems in our own lives? The range is very wide. There is the falling into false roles such as rescuing, subtly perpetrating bias or micro-aggression or overt aggression, overworking, undercharging perhaps because it feels bad to ask for money for help, overcharging because our own lives need the money, false representation of our own expertise either more or less than we actually have, thinking we ought to know and acting like we know because we are expected to know, falling in love and not wanting to admit it, hating and not wanting to admit it...it is a long list of uncomfortable possibilities. I don't think any of us is immune.

You can see that from a psychodynamic origin, my thinking has become not only more relational but also ecological. The things that are the most important aspects of psychotherapy for me today are consistent with a larger ecological view: both the self and the world are constructed through social participation and language. Human communication is a reflexive process in which participants in a relationship dialectically co-create meanings, thereby defining the relationship in particular ways and, in turn, being defined by it (Maddock & Larson, 1995). The process of validating or invalidating as occurs in psychotherapy is a potent example of human communication that seeks to capitalize on this process for both curative and maturational goals.

Try to Make It Real, Compared to What?

Psychotherapists are just people with shortcomings who have training. Sometimes the best of what we have at the time isn't enough. This is hard to confront oneself about. Through training, supervision, and consultation we attempt to eliminate the shortsightedness, emotional blockages, cognitive errors, and limited information to decrease the chance of our shortcomings getting in the way. But, it cannot ever be completely safe for the client. The possibility that we will fail to be curative cannot be entirely eliminated. Yet, I would argue that it is our mistakes and errors that produce some of the most remarkable changes in both participants. In this sense, I would have to say that psychotherapy is not safe, and should not be. Simultaneously, I would hope that the "safety" we offer as psychotherapists is the willingness to truly look at ourselves with the same intensity and honesty with which we look at the client so that we take their reactions seriously as information for ourselves. We can also offer stillness and an opportunity. Wouldn't you say it is fearsome and worthy to offer clear thinking, clear perceiving, and the willingness to speak frankly and clearly, and furthermore, to have as much guts as we ask our clients to have? It really is quite an offer.

To be clear thinking, clear perceiving, and clear talking seems to me to require a lot of experiencing. Experience can come in many forms, such as reading, attending conferences, watching movies, traveling, getting consultation, giving consultation, and stretching the enclosure within which I ordinarily operate. For the experienced psychotherapist, in vivo supervision and exposing the literal dialogue that one has had with clients is likely long past. Letting your work be seen again can be frightening. Perhaps psychoanalysts still practice literal transcription of their sessions for supervision. Everyone should do this now and again. It is too easy in supervision or consultation to only divulge up to a point. It is equally too easy for consultants not to carefully analyze the case material, or to be too quick to take the case material at face value. This seems obvious, but it is easier to support in theory than to actually do. To really push knowledge requires suffering a fair amount of anxiety. It is in our job description to know blind spots, our own and others'; however, it is not much fun in practice.

On Arrogance

Clients, supervisees, and sometimes consultees say that I am blunt. Many say that I am perceptive. Most find me warm but a bit scary, perhaps because I say things they may not have expected to hear. I make mistakes and have had to recant or apologize. Most people appreciate this unless the mistake was too big for them. Mistakes such as these that couldn't get worked out have been few, but they have happened, and I tend not to forget them. They weren't made out of malice. Never. But, they happened probably because of blindness, or blindsidedness, or arrogance. I really thought that I knew. Often, I felt this because a new modality or paradigm in psychotherapeutic technology excited me, and I thought I saw the way. This attitude has in retrospect never served me well.

I think as psychotherapists we all run the risk of being or becoming arrogant about the depth of our own wisdom. We listen to and know about aspects of human life to which most people only want a prurient, limited exposure. We often live there in our professional lives. We are professionally credentialed as seekers of knowledge regarding humans and human behavior. We are elevated in our roles and given access that is privileged. However, this alone doesn't make us wiser. Don't you think that the mantel of wisdom is actually earned in other ways?

Many of us have suffered injustice, malicious intent, and much worse. It is heroic to not become broken; maybe dented, or injured, but not broken. This is truly difficult because there can be such horror perpetrated in life. While none of us is immune to this possibility, in the lives of women and girls, it is not a remote possibility. We all know someone personally who has had such horror perpetrated on them. As psychotherapists with women and girls as clients, we hear such stories regularly. I don't think women heal differently than men, but we are exposed to more molestation, rape, violation of various sorts, and personal injury that are often perpetrated by men. This introduces an element of difference in the experience of women and girls that may be shared by gay men, but different than heterosexual men. For if we accept the supposition that women and girls are more relational by nature and we suffer the majority of relational violations, then where does that leave us? It leaves us running into a wall, over and again because we cannot embrace a relational life without risking vulnerability to violation. While empathy, understanding, and a sense of safety from being dismissed and judged are crucial to healing, more is needed.

With no intention of minimizing the facts of female vulnerability, I still say this: *resist becoming broken.* We must not abandon our will and the ability to still become more. Do not forget the many identities that we all have within us and use them in support of our better selves. In my personal life I tried to do many things to safeguard myself and my loved ones. Those who would do harm sometimes got in anyway. Why does this happen? It just does because those who intend harm find their opportunities. If I could undo time I would, but in the absence of that power, I urge us all to resist feeling and being broken. Do not see yourself as broken. You can be at fault in some way, or have made mistakes, and still, do not become broken.

A Perversion of the Victim State

This is my rant. In my mind a regretful social development now soils the dialogue about victimization and the social remedies for it. I have seen many instances in which elements within our culture have co-opted the voice of victims which gave rise to the civil rights and the women's liberation movements (forgive me if I fail to mention other important victim advocacy movements), and turned it into the rhetoric of disingenuous victimhood in which declarations of being "offended" is intended to trump any further conversation. When a significant wage discrepancy persists between women and men for the identical job especially in the highest ranks of corporate governance, and when among university faculty women with doctorates earn up to $16,600 less per year than their male counterparts and are less likely to get promoted to full professorship to boot (Claudio Sanchez, NPR News, September 15, 2010), and limits on access and opportunities persist for most people of color in the United States, charges of "reverse discrimination" are mostly disingenuous. When a climate of competition to stake rights as victims arises, an ugly tangent emerges that is opportunistic, riding the backs of movements that called out long-standing oppressions which, on the basis of unfounded prejudice, deny basic rights and fairness to populations which have done nothing to earn such censure. Instead, in these distorted interactions, adopting the voice of a victim and crying offense is meant to silence anyone who is hurting our feelings and gives a pass from self-confrontation. Regardless of one's color, class, gender, nation of origin, etc., it is possible to employ the concept of victimization opportunistically, therefore, as a ploy. This was never the intent in giving voice to those who have been victim to various crimes and/or oppressed by gender, sexual preference, racial, and class politics.

However, when the tactic has worked, as it has in our culture, and has found social validation, it has become difficult to speak out in instances where there is perversion of the notion of "blaming the victim." How do we manage the morass inherent in determining who speaks authentically of having been victimized, and who seeks to use victimization language to avoid needed confrontation? How can we circumnavigate the tendency on the part of some to feel justified in elevating brokenness and still simultaneously insist on the rights of victims to voice their pain and circumstances? This is not an easy or foolproof task and is particularly hard when it happens in the psychotherapy interaction, which is one that by definition should be empathic to victims. Perhaps an antidote lies again in establishing the goal in psychotherapy of bringing the best self forward in each of us, and by envisioning first "healing," then "thriving." Hurt, injured, wronged, blamed, offended, humiliated, unjustly judged, oppressed, denied of opportunities, neglected, abandoned, and persecuted . . . all these things happen and can break us if the circumstances are such. These are certainly wrongs, sins, if you like in some instances. Still, we should ask, "What is the route to thriving, not just healing?" This question insists on movement past and through victimization and victimhood. In addition, I would like to bring back the word "power." We don't like that word anymore. It is identified with the aggressor and used synonymous with "control." However, let's not let the pejorative use in the current vernacular (which is closely allied with the ploy of crying victim) appropriate a word and a concept that is vital to thriving. Using common dictionary definitions, Maddock and Larsen (1995) writes:

> Power is the capacity to influence. Power is the energy of life, literally and figuratively moving out and taking up space in the world. Control can be defined most simply as a reciprocal to power, that is, as the capacity to restrain or regulate influence. Control is the boundedness of life, recognized in the inevitable limitations on everything that exists. (p. 55)

These are two aspects of a continuum, neither of which is wrong nor right, but which exist by laws of nature in constant dynamic tension. We need both as a society and culture, and we each as individuals need both. Power and control are not political or social-justice swear words. Rather, these words describe the ebb and flow of the dynamics of change and resistance to change. I think for women and girls who have been victims, responsible, ethical use of power is particularly transformative. In the case of victim criers, regardless of gender, color, class, etc., the misuse of both power and control will be a focus of the therapy since the co-opting of power is part of the problem. A relentless focus on the emergence of the best self and notions of personal integrity would be indispensible in both cases because whether victimized or stuck in victimhood, a transition is necessary. My fervent hope is, that as women and as psychotherapists we will resist the co-opting of victimization into victimhood and we will begin to right the tilt caused by the various "–isms" rather than to tilt the balance differently. This borders on the spiritual and religious.

Everything That Rises Must Converge

Pierre Teilhard de Chardin, a well-traveled Jesuit priest, scientist, and philosopher, born in 1881, conceived of a notion, the "Omega Point," which was published in the 1950s. A part of it says (Chardin, p. 11): "Remain true to yourself, but move ever upward toward greater consciousness and greater love! At the summit you will find yourselves united with all those who, from every direction, have made the same ascent. For everything that rises must converge."

This last sentence was later used by Flannery O'Connor as the title of a book of short stories, published posthumously in 1965, featuring a short story of the same title about racism and moral failings of the soul. I saw the phrase again, in Danzy Senna's novel, Caucasia, published in 1999. It is a lovely phrase in my mind. While I don't share Teilhard de Chardin's and O'Connor's Catholic and Christian religious background, I share the optimistic spiritual tone that these words impart. In many ways, psychotherapy is like this too. It may sound too lofty, but we have only to see how ubiquitous some ideas that originated in the psychotherapeutic field have become culturally accepted and used. This is a power to be taken seriously and used in the best possible ways. It is for these reasons that I think psychotherapy in the United States can no longer be easily separated from notions of social justice. It is obvious from the previous paragraphs that to accept shared responsibility for the development of a better self is a spiritual undertaking because we aim for a better world. When we begin to take our influence seriously, because we accept the goals to guide and accompany personal change in people, and because some of these people are influential and even if they are not, the changes among many people will be influential, what we do cannot be easily separated from the spiritual either. So, it would be important to guide wisely and well.

There is more left out of these pages than I could possibly recount and more people than I could mention who belong to this story, and to whom I owe a large debt of gratitude. I really do believe in the Unbroken Chain of those, both known to me and unknown, who believed in me, supported me, and potentiated my being a better person. I pass on my best self to those I love and to those on whose behalf I work so that they might do the same...so that they might reach that which they love and might not have to work quite as hard, but just hard enough to know their own achievement. I dream of a convergence, sometime in the far off distance, each of us having made the ascent.

Acknowledgments: Many thanks to Flora and Marie, my stalwarts; to David, Jim, and Laura, my mentors; Lillian and Marcella for believing, and to M.A.M., the loves of my life.

References

American Psychological Association. (2009). Workforce Studies. http://www.apa.org/workforce/publications/09-member/table-01.pdf.

Cozolino, L. (2002). *The neuroscience of psychotherapy: Building and rebuilding the human brain.* New York, NY: W. W. Norton & Co.

Maddock, J. W., & Larson, N. R. (1995). *Incestuous families: An ecological approach to understanding and treatment.* New York: W. W. Norton & Co.

Maturana, H. R., & Varela, F. J. (1991). *Autopoiesis and cognition: The realization of the living.* Boston: Springer Publications.

O'Connor, F. (1965). *Everything that rises must converge.* New York: Farrar, Strauss, & Giroux.

Sanchez, C. (September 15, 2010). Women outnumber men earning doctoral degrees. NPR News, *Morning Edition.*

Schnarch, D. (1991). *The sexual crucible: An integration of sexual and marital therapy.* New York: W. W. Norton & Co.

Senna, D. (1999). *Caucasia.* New York: Riverhead Books.

Teilhard de Chardin, P. (1959). *The phenomenon of man.* New York: Harper Perennial.

Trimble, J. E. (2007). Prolegomena for the connotations of construct use in the measurement of ethnic and racial identity. *Journal of Counseling Psychology, 54*(3), 247–258.

Yeats, W. B. (1893, 1902). Earth, fire, and water. In *The Celtic twilight* (p. 136). Retrieved February 13, 2011, from http://www.sacred-texts.com/neu/yeats/twi/twi24.htm and www.gutenberg.org/cache/epub/10459/pg10459.html.

Adversity, Healing, and the Development and Practice of a Woman Psychologist

11

JENNIFER RUFF

IN THE 1960S IN THE PROJECTS in the Bronx, the notion of growing up to become a doctor of any kind was not one which most of us entertained, especially not us little girls. My earliest thoughts about a future vocation were focused however around work as a healer. Having been exposed to what I envisioned as the magnificent healing abilities of Florence Nightingale in my grade school history books, I romanticized her as an angel of mercy who could heal and comfort hundreds of soldiers in their darkest hours. So, when asked by my mother what I wanted to be when I grew up, I readily replied that I might like to become a nurse. I explained how I wanted to help sick people heal and thought that becoming a nurse might be a reasonable and appropriate goal. My mother replied that although this was a fine idea, if it was treating and healing the sick that interested me, I could also consider becoming a doctor. Really? I could? *A girl? From the projects?* The seed was planted, but it would be many years before it took root.

I suspect that in general the passion in the art (and science) of healing for many has been sparked by their own problems and the journeys traversed in finding some acceptable resolution of, or peacemaking with, those problems. Often, it is thusly that the Wounded Healer comes into being. Pope & Feldman-Summers (1992) reported in a national survey of 250 male and 250 female psychologists that 69.3% of women and 32.85% of men reported having experienced physical or sexual abuse. In another study, Pope and Tabachnick (1994) found that 400 of 476 therapists had themselves been in therapy and 70% indicated that therapy should be required in psychology graduate schools. Kaslow and Friedman (as cited in Pope & Tabachnick, 1994) found that 13 of 14 clinical psychology students who were in therapy while in training ranked personal treatment second only to clinical practice as having the most influence on their development as clinicians, outranking supervision, academic course work, and outside readings.

I have been aware for some time that my own desire to become a healer originated in part from early painful life experiences. However, it was due to the healing experiences that followed and the transformative changes that would come about as a result, that I decided to pursue a career as a psychologist.

Adversity

As a child, my home was sometimes filled with violence. Violence entered in the form of unpredictable fits of rage in which everything the abuser hated about himself, triggered by some unknown event and mixed with alcohol, was unleashed in our home in torrents of fury. Episodes of physical abuse were accompanied by scathing verbal assaults which seemed designed to destroy the core of one's being, causing even more damage than physical violence could, instead inflicting a spiritual violence on the young souls entrusted to the abuser's care. I was spared direct physical and the worst of the verbal abuse during these episodes. However, I recall the helplessness with which I bore witness to these events and vicariously took on the pain of the victim. So I was also a survivor. As survivors often do, over time I became unaware of the undercurrent of pain caused by the rage and violence, and immersed myself in the "doing" of my life. In "doing" I found distraction, and I would also nourish gifts that would provide me with hope and empowerment.

I say that spiritual violence was done. Believing that hope, meaning, and purpose in one's life are primary guiding and grounding forces, and as a Christian woman who now experiences God's love, the death of the possibility of finding those transcendent dimensions of life is surely one of the hardest consequences of trauma from which one can recover. It is the death of the spiritual child.

My mother was bright, had some college education at the time she married my father, and would probably have been considered a feminist. However, I wondered at the mixed messages about women's roles that I interpreted from my mother's modeling. While encouraging me to have the highest professional goals that need not be limited due to my female gender, as well as supporting my intellectual development as a female, which was as important than that of men, she herself did not feel sufficiently empowered to protect herself or her children by removing us from harm for many years. In contrast, my father was terrified of his sons being "weak" and he chose violence as the method of ensuring this would not occur. He also had ideas that women should be primarily concerned with their sex appeal. Other talents or gifts that women had were ignored, deemed unimportant, or demeaned if perceived as a threat. He and my mother made an odd couple indeed.

At some point in elementary school, my intelligence was tested and I was labeled a "gifted" child. Subsequently I was enrolled in an advanced academic program for gifted children which provided me the opportunity for greater intellectual creativity at an accelerated pace. More importantly to me, the program provided a distraction from events at home. I was in heaven. I lost myself in my schoolwork. That I was intellectually gifted *and* a female was not threatening to anyone there. I will always remember Mr. Weinberg, my elementary school science teacher, who recognized and encouraged my talent, even though he was a man and I just a little girl. He and a favorite uncle provided me with a glimpse of healthy masculinity, in which children were treated with loving kindness. I flourished in that environment.

For my first science project, I dissected and compared several animal brains to the human brain (although the school generosity stopped here, I had to diagram that!) in terms of structure and function from an evolutionary perspective. I realized in hindsight that the project was a cover for my real interest; I was looking for concrete explanations for behavior. Not wanting to believe that people could be responsible for the cruelty I had seen, I initially rejected the participation of free will in those behaviors and looked for structures that once identified as pathological in form or function, would then fully explain how these occurrences could happen. It was much preferable to the truth.

As a young child, I developed a growing belief in God, that he was everywhere, and that he was loving and kind, despite some poor representation within the Catholic school I attended for a short period of time. In fact, some undeveloped idea of his transcendence, especially of all that was wrong in the world, sustained me through some very difficult times. That the God of the New Testament, and indeed much of the scriptures themselves, reflected a patriarchal society did not matter to me. In fact, God as loving, kind, and understanding while being omniscient, omnipresent, and omnipotent, *and* male may have represented the balance I needed to some of the toxic masculinity to which I was exposed. Rather, I understand "him" to embody both feminine and masculine traits. I also understood Jesus to be humble and particularly kind to women in the stories of the New Testament. Images of him washing the feet of the disciples, his extension of compassion towards the adulteress, and his friendship with Mary Magdalene predominated and I chose those as the images that would color my understanding of him as a child. Nevertheless, as my helplessness grew, eventually I would turn my back even on him.

My parents divorced just prior to my completion of elementary school and events led us to move to rural Kansas. Now bored, unchallenged, and full of unresolved pain from which I had no distraction, I gave in to the more powerful feeling of anger. Later, I dropped out of college and eventually moved to Los Angeles. I disavowed stereotypic female traits such as patience, empathy, sensitivity, the nurturance of relationships, whether with God or other people, and separated myself from my own experience of vulnerable emotions. Instead, I embraced autonomy as a form of protection, cutting myself off from vulnerable feelings and meaningful relationships, denying even myself compassion and optimism, believing in neither, and presenting a tough exterior to the world. I lived in the moment, trapped in a protective cocoon of anger and denial and there I resided for several years. Eventually, I looked around at what my life had become and was far from pleased. I lacked direction, goals, keenly felt the wasting of my potential and of the time given me, and was predictably unfulfilled in intimate relationships.

Healing and Spiritual Optimism

From within the wreckage that I had created of my life, I began to consider change. First, I began to read the Bible in search of answers. I needed to frame my life in the context of transcendent meaning and purpose to motivate me towards change. So, I studied and I talked with God. Our conversations were personal and as my understanding of his omniscience grew, I felt free in expressing a full range of emotion, including for a time, fully directing my anger at him personally. Eventually, I made a decision. I asked for liberation from the life that I had chosen before and now seemed stuck in, and it was given me. I simply stopped behaviors to which I had succumbed for years, some which were reinforcing to my wounded status. The inner healing would take some years to come, but it was through those sometimes painful and sometimes transformative experiences that I would begin to develop in wholeness as a woman, and that I began my development as a healer.

While the stirrings of these changes began, I worked in the telecommunications industry, working my way up to corporate account executive positions. Initially, I enjoyed the world of hardware, software, and the latest in telecommunications technology. This male-dominated world was also about "doing" and initially it was a great fit for me. Given sufficient autonomy and power to bring about resolutions for my clients, I excelled. Reinforcement was immediately evident in client retention and sales, as well as my paycheck. However, once the thrill of success died down, I began to feel that my professional life was stale. Although networking and building relationships were a significant part of my work, they were superficial. The joy I was beginning to feel at creating a new life for myself seemed to fall flat when facing reams of spreadsheets, mounds of technology, and playing politics in the corporate world.

Early in those years, I began psychotherapy with a wonderfully warm and empathic female marriage and family therapist. I began the exploration, experiencing, and processing of emotions thus far avoided. Insights gained, emotions felt, validated, and normalized, and the development of compassion and forgiveness in addition to a growing spiritual optimism, provided the platform from which I was able to make profound change. Creativity in healing was encouraged by my therapist, and my pursuit of the transcendent, meaning, and purpose were supported. In developing my faith in God as my relationship with him grew, I was free to choose an attitude of hope for my life.

This seemingly simple change in orientation dramatically changed my life. I no longer saw what I was helpless to change, but that over which I had influence. Looking around the world with new perspective, I was astounded at the possibilities. I also believed that because I had a relationship with God, that if there was such a thing as destiny in individual life purpose, it would be made known to me. In the meantime, my everyday life had already taken on new meaning and purpose as I embraced each day and the unknown future, this time rich with possibility.

At this time, I had dreams with fantastic imagery that represented the progression of these inner changes. One recurring series of dreams began with terrifying images of the end of the world, in which tidal waves would come and overtake the land and everyone on it. I never ran from the wave, but walked toward it knowing I had to go with a feeling of dread. Those dreams changed over many months, reflecting the changes in my orientation to life. Eventually, no longer (spiritually) overwhelming, the waves, although deadly, ceased to be frightening. My fear was replaced with curiosity. There was something alluring about death. In one memorable dream image, I stood next to the wall of water as it rose motionless beside me, higher than my eye could follow. Its stillness was expectant as it beckoned. I plunged into the water and was instantly transformed. I had become a spot of color, and floated upwards weightless on a current that was neither air nor water. Looking around, I saw that there were countless other spots of color, each different from the next, and each float weaving its way upwards, shimmering and expectant. The beauty of the scene and the experience that it evoked defy words. However, within that experience, possibilities, love, transformation, and the transcendent were alive.

At that time in my life I was in the process of moving from my identity as a wounded survivor in an existential vacuum to developing wholeness in spiritual and psychological optimism. I was ravenous for that which was edifying. I read psychology and self-help books about adults abused as children, adult children of alcoholics, depression, anger, anything that seemed relevant. I continued in psychotherapy, attended to my health through exercise, studied religious and spiritual teachings including Eastern meditation and yoga, put new insights into practice in my life and relationships, and was always aware of God's transcendent and loving presence.

I know the power of the resources to which I had availed myself. More importantly, I intimately know the ability of the human spirit to survive and thrive in the face of adversity. Victor Frankl, the father of logotherapy, in *Man's Search for Meaning* (1963) noted that this occurs when one exercises the right to "choose one's attitude in any given set of circumstances, to chose one's own way" (p. 104). I had chosen my way. Over time I began to feel strongly that there was some other meaning that I could, perhaps was meant to, bring out of my early life experiences and some purpose for which I could use it in the world. Bengali poet and author Rabindranath Tagore (1916) says it beautifully:

> The pain was great when the strings
> Were being tuned, my Master!
> Begin your music, and let me forget the
> Pain, let me feel in beauty that you had
> In your mind through those pitiless days

At some point on this path, my therapist wondered whether I would be interested in becoming a therapist myself. I only stopped to wonder why this had not occurred to me before.

Back to School and Choosing a Theoretical Orientation

Soon thereafter, I returned to school with the goal of beginning my work towards a PhD in Clinical Psychology. As a divorced woman in my thirties in urban Los Angeles with a mortgage and bills to pay, I considered the sacrifices that I would make in returning to school and beginning a new career. First, a career change meant a significant pay reduction for at least a few years, and the hours would be long as I would have to work full-time while accruing practicum, internship, and research hours. Most importantly, I knew that I risked giving up motherhood. The conviction that it was the right choice for me reigned and I re-entered the world of education with delight.

As I reached the graduate level in my academic career, it became of significant importance to choose a theoretical orientation. While my spiritual and existential leanings played a significant role in my own healing and development, I was initially impressed by the support for cognitive behavioral therapy (CBT), particularly in the treatment of anxiety and depression. I found the structure and relatively linear approach to change in CBT both appealing and accessible. I also related personally to how powerful changing one's thinking could be in changing one's life. While I worked to master the techniques of CBT, the importance of the relationship as primary in healing emerged. Indeed, Aaron Beck, a father of cognitive behavioral therapy, emphasized the collaborative relationship as a necessary condition for the success of CBT. In the context of that collaboration and an ever-developing approach of acceptance and positive regard ala Carl Rogers, I began my practice of psychotherapy.

Soon, my experience of CBT was that it simply did not fit all problems or all patients. Clearly, schema and core beliefs develop in the context of early life experiences and are influenced by the way one constructs her worldview based on those experiences. Moreover, while I believed that change does not occur merely as a result of insight and without the benefit of action—often made accessible by CBT—I knew that insight into the inner workings of the subconscious was extremely important. As such I found a need for increased understanding of the dynamics of the subconscious to complement and inform any action plan. Also, patients with characterological disorders often simply did not "collaborate" with CBT approaches. Last, I could not help but recognize common existential themes in those core beliefs (annihilation, meaninglessness, etc.). So I began to see the three schools of psychology as complementary and inextricably linked. I was challenged to enhance my skills and expand my understanding and use of other theoretical orientations and subsequently read and obtained supervision in other theories including Adlerian, Kohutian, Jungian and Frankl's logotherapy.

While not a part of my graduate training sadly, it was clear that my patient's spiritual and religious beliefs were often worthy of exploration. As such, I sought independent training to guide my efforts in that part of my work when clinically appropriate. I am always interested in if and how my patient's spiritual or religious beliefs may influence him. Does he believe in a transcendent deity, subscribe to a religion or spiritual practice? How do those beliefs impact the way problems, symptoms, or relationships are approached? If he does believe in God, is God punishing and malevolent or loving and full of grace? Exploration of those beliefs in respectful context of the patient's background is often helpful, and I sometimes make referrals to the appropriate spiritual leaders or to one's scripture for clarification. Does the patient have some ideas about the meaning and purpose of life in general, and specifically about her own life? Patients have often remarked that they are surprised when I ask about their spiritual lives, saying that they often assume that we as psychologists "don't believe in that kind of thing."

Being a Woman Psychologist in a Man's Prison

My areas of clinical specialty have been determined by interests that I developed over time. I feel most professionally challenged and fulfilled when working with patients who have struggled with adversity, substance abuse and addiction, histories of abuse, depression and anxiety, chronic pain, and with incarcerated persons. With the possibility of student loan repayment and some interest in working with incarcerated patients after having worked with dually diagnosed parolees, I accepted a job working in a prison for men in California. I also work part-time at the University of California, San Francisco as faculty teaching third year medical residents in Family and Community Medicine. Starkly contrasting positions, I am never bored. In order to reflect on my experiences as a woman psychologist, it is easiest to do so in the context of my current primary occupation.

Within the prison, I work with patients in a housing unit commonly referred to by inmates as "the hole." In order to be assigned housing there, inmates have been deemed a threat to the safety and security of the institution due to in-prison behavior, usually of a violent nature or by association with prison gangs. Handcuffed or waist-chained inmates are escorted to sessions by two custody officers and therapy is conducted in rooms in which inmates sit in steel "therapy modules," padlocked closed and bolted into the concrete floor beneath them. The therapy environment itself is unique and a constant reminder about the dangerousness of some of the inmates there. As one might imagine, female clinicians working in male prisons, and particularly in housing units designed for the highest level inmates such as these, are faced with other unique challenges.

First, we look different than the majority of other females who work there and are dressed in custody "greens" like their male counterparts, rendered almost genderless by design. By comparison female clinicians wear street clothes and more closely resemble females on the outside. Many of my patients are "lifers" and as such may not again see or experience women in the ways they had while on the streets. With strict over-familiarity rules in the prison, female clinicians particularly are tasked with differentiating between true clinical transference and inappropriate and manipulative behavior. Genital exposure and masturbation to female staff (and more recently male staff) have become common and a problem with which custody and mental health staff continues to struggle.

As women clinicians, it is necessary to protect the female side of ourselves that is so unlike the toxic masculine values and behaviors to which many there subscribe. Unfortunately, many of these inmates exemplify pathological masculinity, whether as the result of their upbringing and male modeling in the home and their neighborhoods, or because of the challenges faced in the harsh reality of prison life. Terry Kupers (2005) posits that gender differences are intensified within prisons, and he describes toxic masculinity as "the constellation of socially regressive male traits that serve to foster domination, the devaluation of women, homophobia, and wanton violence" (p. 714). Having spent some time and effort recapturing and embracing the inner female qualities necessary for my own healing including sensitivity, patience, and compassion, I sometimes find those qualities viewed with suspicion, as evidence of weakness, or threatened by those who would seek to manipulate them. Kupers goes on to note that "toxic masculinity also includes a strong measure of the male proclivities that lead to resistance in psychotherapy" (p. 714).

To assist in meeting the challenges of this work, I make regular use of the resources available including supportive collegial relationships and readily accessible clinical consultation. As a woman psychologist exposed to toxic masculinity early in life, awareness of transference and countertransference issues is crucial and necessary in keeping the clinical needs of my patients primary, while protecting the personal and female part of me that willingly risks vulnerability for a deeper and more meaningful life. However, my early life experience also informs my understanding of many of my patients. Most of my patients were victims of abuse as children and exposed to violence throughout their lives. As a result of my experiences, I am able to more fully empathize with theirs. I understand how the aggrandizement of stereotypical traits can evolve from an insider's perspective, and maybe a more comprehensive vantage point. I know intimately the need to balance healing from the past with responsibility for one's behavior past, present, and future. Last and maybe most importantly, I have an idea of what the process of healing is like from that inside position and from there feel a genuine empathy and compassion that I believe positively impacts our relationship and the patient's work in therapy.

As a woman working with men who are more likely than noncriminal men to value stereotypical masculine traits in general, I find myself having to work harder and be more creative in my clinical work with them. It is a challenge to balance the knowledge that gender stereotypes are exemplified in prison with an open approach to my patients as individuals. Having said that, as a female clinician working with this population I have had to educate myself about how to recognize disorders that may present differently in men than in women, as well as how to treat them in ways that reduce resistance to therapy. Emotional issues are typically underreported by males, and likely more so by incarcerated males, who view mental health problems as a weakness (Kupers, 2005). As such they often do not request and even refuse services from which they could benefit. When male inmate patients do participate in therapy, they are less likely to use emotional language, preferring instead to describe behaviors and share narratives, and their demand for respect is primary. I have had generally good response to the use of empathy and compassion, and empathic confrontation when appropriate, in a way that doesn't threaten their self-esteem. I continue to develop my expertise in working with them.

Although the majority of male prison staff members with whom I work are respectful and friendly, toxic masculinity unfortunately exists and even thrives within some of them as well. As mental health clinicians we naturally care about our patients and as part of our clinical work we ask them how they feel, we extend compassion, we nurture and guide their motivation for change, and we reinforce their successes. This has earned us the title of "thug huggers" with some custody and even medical staff.

Women in this environment may experience sexism in the form of denigrating gender "jokes" by male staff. At least several times I have been "kidded" about being "a blonde" to diminish some point I am making in conversation with custody staff, and even once by a male mental health professional in the middle of a clinical case consultation. While already working with a population with very complex pathology, challenges that arise with staff that stem from sexism can be difficult to navigate.

However, as noted, most of my colleagues and coworkers are respectful, and some even appreciative and supportive of what we do. The presence and increase in mental health services are credited with contributing to decreases in violence and "cell extractions," in which full tactical gear and strategies are used to extract a noncompliant inmate from his cell. It was no small recognition one day when leaving a unit that a male custody officer stopped me to say "I just wanted to say thank you for what you do here. It gives these guys some relief and it's appreciated."

Thoughts on the Art and Science of Therapy for Future Women Healers

I believe that my patients have their own answers. The *science* of psychology changes and research often seems inconsistent. The *art* of therapy however lies within the creativity of the therapist as the *agent* of change to assist the patient in finding what is already there, and by use of the relationship as the *vehicle* by which healing occurs.

In relation to women as therapist healers, we have significant contributions to make to the healing process. Women are tasked with bringing life into the world. As women therapists, I see a natural extension of this role in the healing of wounds that life often brings. Also, few would argue that women are inclined towards and thrive on emotional connectedness with others. Perhaps due to this proclivity, whether through socialization or genetics, qualities important in the therapeutic relationship such as compassion, sensitivity, patience, and empathy, are readily developed. Last, as a result of thousands of years of oppression as women, we may be uniquely qualified to be present within reparative relationships with others in the midst of their suffering. For instance, women may be more comfortable entering the dark cave of the depressed patient's world, remaining there with them if necessary, but from the vantage point of our own health, healing, and clinical acumen, hold within the light with which to illuminate that which the patient may currently be unable to see on her own.

I have been practicing clinical work a mere eight years. I have learned much in that period of time, but embrace the knowledge that my development as a clinician is a lifelong endeavor. In considering what counsel

I would give other women choosing to become psychotherapists, I offer several suggestions.

First, thoughtfully consider the motivation for your career choice. Know whether you are internally and/or externally motivated towards the profession, particularly if you intend to obtain your doctorate. The sacrifice and commitment are substantial. In the end, my return to school meant waiting many years to get married again, and the opportunity to have children came and went, although I now have two wonderful stepsons. It is important to consider these significant life choices and develop a realistic plan to meet the challenges ahead.

Be aware of your background, experiences, biases, and gifts as a woman, and attend to other cultural nuances such as those that arise from your membership in ethnic, racial, religious, or spiritual groups, or your gender identification or sexual orientation. Acknowledge how your worldview informs your interactions with your patients. Maintain awareness, educate yourself, and practice your skills in respecting both your cultural identity and that of your patients.

Acknowledge and treat the "impostor phenomenon" if necessary. As a high-achieving woman it is not uncommon to feel that one is "not bright, capable or creative, despite ample evidence to the contrary" (Imes & Rose Clance, 1984, p. 69). This may interfere with your goals as well as leaving you feeling disempowered. As a high-achieving woman, you may have been labeled as the 'bright" child in the family and expectations of your success may have seemed to devalue the hard work required to achieve it. As you enter a world filled with other bright high-achievers, you may be left feeling paralyzed when faced with projects if you self-impose perfectionist expectations while devaluing your capabilities. Suzanne Imes and Pauline Rose Clance (1984) recommend treatment for this impostor phenomenon.

Be aware of your wounds. Know yourself well and do your own healing work. Everyone has the need for healing. You deserve healing as much as the patients you want to serve, and they and you will be the better for it if you are clear about this before beginning clinical work. You may hear that countertransference is clinically informative. I would add that its occurrence should be a cue to remind you of your own wounds as countertransference often happens as the patient's wounds touch your own.

Study and practice at least one theoretical orientation well, but don't be a purist. You will become frustrated and will do your patients a disservice. Read the research and pursue what works, but never forget that you are the tool and the relationship is the vehicle by which healing occurs, and that the patient in the room with you is not a subject in a research study, but a person. As such she, like you, is unlikely to fit perfectly into any one mold.

Honor your patients and what is required of them to sit with you, tell their stories, and share their experiences with you. Honor their pain. Sometimes, regardless of your theoretical orientation, the most respectful and appropriate thing you can do when faced with someone's pain, is to give silent witness to it.

I have heard it said that mechanics drive the worst cars. Take time for yourself and practice self-care. There is something unique and beautiful about women healers in their generosity of spirit and their sometimes tireless commitment to the art of healing. Across culture and time, women have put themselves second to the needs of others as primary caregivers, sacrificing their capacities to create, to become, to realize, and achieve their individual potential apart from that done in the service of others. Think about the gifts that you have been given that led you towards healing and allow you to practice the art of healing. With gratitude and appreciation, care for yourself as much as you would for your patients.

Looking Back and Looking Ahead

Obviously not all patients are especially motivated, insightful, or ready for change. We may even be taken advantage of by those we seek to serve, and sometimes the work can be discouraging. However, some of the most courageous people I have known in my life are also numbered amongst the patients with whom I have worked. They are those who despite sometimes tremendous obstacles and histories of adversity and trauma, nevertheless find the spark and the inner resources necessary to ignite movement towards change. I consider it an honor when that patient allows me into his inner world and I am rewarded by movement that occurs as a result of his initiative. So, that my work is professionally fulfilling is unquestionable.

When I first considered whether to move into the field of psychology, and now when I consider whether it was the right choice, I think about how I might look back on my life in later years. In looking ahead in this way, I am guided to make important life choices by my most primary desire to believe in the end that I have participated in my life fully and in a meaningful way. I believe that I will feel satisfied that I have done so. As such, and even considering the sacrifices made, I would do it all over again.

References

Frankl, V. E. (1963). *Man's search for meaning*. Boston: Beacon Press.

Imes, S., & Rose Clance, P. (1984). Treatment of the impostor phenomenon in high-achieving women. In C. M. Brody (Ed.), *Women therapists working with women*, vol. 7. New York: Springer Publishing Company.

Kupers, T.A. (2005). Toxic masculinity as a barrier to mental health treatment in prison. *Journal of Clinical Psychology. 61*(6). 713–724.

Pope, K., & Feldman-Summers, S. (1992). National survey of psychologists' sexual and physical abuse history and their evaluation of training and competence in these areas. *Professional Psychology: Research and Practice. 23*(5), 353–361.

Pope, K., & Tabachnick, B.G. (1994). Therapists as patients: A national survey of psychologists' experiences, problems, and beliefs. *Professional Psychology: Research and Practice. 25*(3), 247–258.

Tagore, R. (1916). *The fruit gathering*. Project Gutenberg. New York: The MacMillan Company. Retrieved February 13, 2011 from netlibrary, http://www.gutenberg.org/ebooks/6522.

Conclusion
Women of Words: Psychotherapy from a Feminine Perspective

LILLIAN COMAS-DÍAZ AND MARCELLA BAKUR WEINER

THE 11 CONTRIBUTORS IN THIS ANTHOLOGY are women of words, women of wisdom. As psychotherapist-healers, they contribute to the feminization of psychotherapy. This process seems consistent with the assertion that the original shamans were females (Davis-Kimball, 2002). Like their foremothers, these women psychotherapists heal from a feminine approach. But what is healing from a feminine perspective? According to Kakar (1985) the essential characteristics for healing, such as nurturance, intuition, concern, and connectedness, are inherently feminine. Likewise, in her edited book *Women as Therapists*, Dorothy Cantor (1990) argues for understanding the psychotherapeutic experience from a feminine perspective.

The essays in this anthology show us what it is like to heal from a female perspective. As they shared their personal and professional journeys, the contributors revealed who the women psychotherapists are. They narrate how they became psychotherapists, how they practice, and eventually, how they evolved as healers. In doing so, they explored the intersection of womanhood, gendered experiences, and spirituality. These stories document a female healing journey. The curative components of such journey include awakening, connectedness, empowerment, holism, and commitment.

Awakening

The contributors to this volume experienced an awakening. This process entailed an awareness of the early circumstances surrounding what it is to be a woman psychotherapist. Some of these influential factors include family of origin, the decision to become a psychotherapist, and the experience of woundedness.

Reflecting upon upbringing, the contributors noted the influence their family of origin exerted over them. Several women, like Thema Bryant-Davis, commented on the sustained emotional support that parents provided. For Marcella Bakur Weiner, home was a playground. Similarly, Beverly Greene remembered that she grew up in a multigenerational household full of humor and playfulness where females had a central role. Carla Bradshaw described her grandmother as being "magical, solid, and soft."

Several women in this collection received complex messages around gender roles. Lillian Comas-Díaz contrasted her grandparents' liberal relationship with her parents' traditional marriage. Jennifer Ruff observed that her father's behavior was stereotypically male, and she wondered about her mother's mixed messages regarding women's roles. Moreover, other women psychotherapists reported receiving conflicted messages about gender roles. Pratyusha (Usha) Tummala-Narra stated that after her arrival to the United States, her parents displayed unequal gender treatment when they restricted her freedom in dating, as opposed to her brother, who was afforded more independence. Similarly, Lillian Comas-Díaz experienced her father's favoritism towards her brother solely due to his gender. Although Patricia Pitta noted that she used to cook with her father, she disclosed that her parents' marital relationship was filled with much love as well as conflict, and consequently, informed her decision to become a psychotherapist.

The women examined how they became psychotherapists. Beverly Fauman, the daughter of a physician, asserted that she did not have a choice—she had to become a psychiatrist. Along these lines, Carla Bradshaw believed that she was fated to become a therapist and cited an "alchemical influence of people who both loved and hated" her, as a major influence. Likewise, Cinzia Levalds stated that the career chose her. She explained that as a child she was told that she had the gift of compassion and empathy. On the other hand, Patricia Pitta discussed how she became a psychologist by accident, later to embrace her profession by choice. While Jennifer Ruff decided to become a psychologist out of her personal healing process; Janice Crawford identified her decision out of soul Braille—she became a psychotherapist by a process of feeling her way along. Similarly, Usha Tummala-Narra became a psychologist as a way of finding meaning out of her dualistic existence, one that reflected her struggle between traditional and progressive notions of being female and Indian.

Some contributors identified a healing legacy. For instance, Lillian Comas-Díaz disclosed that her female ancestors were psychic. Beverly Greene revealed that her great-grandmother was a slave who became a midwife. Thema Bryant-Davis observed that her parents are liberation theology ministers and church leaders who taught her the importance of empowerment and community service. Marcella Bakur Weiner stated that she became a healer after she found her true self. She observed that psychotherapists tend to be individuals who have been cast at a young age into the role of helper in their families. Several of the contributors were helpers or *parentified* children. Several of these helpers carried wounds.

Indeed, the experience of woundedness was prevalent among the women psychotherapists in this collection. Such experience seemed to initiate their need to heal and to be healed. Woundedness took diverse forms among the contributors. Janice Crawford's mother's clinical depression and anxiety led her to distance herself from her mother. Jennifer Ruff's father was physically and emotionally abusive towards her siblings. Consequently, Jennifer experienced vicarious domestic trauma until her parents divorced. She concluded that such trauma and violence could result in the death of the spiritual child. A mixed race woman, Carla Bradshaw stated that her parents succumbed under the pressure of being a multiethnic family. They divorced, and subsequently, Carla moved several times during childhood. As she faced multiple losses, Carla revealed that she learned to listen and remain silent.

Similarly, Lillian Comas-Díaz struggled with speech difficulties as a child, and learned to bond with people in pain—her woundedness spoke to their woundedness. Marcella Bakur Weiner was hospitalized due to an insidious blood infection after a routine tonsillectomy, and was not expected to live. She was bedridden until she was about five years old and reported that she learned how to be alone with her self and comforted. While Beverly Fauman lost her mother at age 15 as a senior in high school, Cinzia Levalds' mother died when she was in graduate school. For both of these women, losing their mother at an early age left a profound impact.

Another type of woundedness came in the form of political unrest. Usha Tummala-Narra's family suffered political violence and trauma after members of a different Indian cast set on fire Usha's maternal grandparents' house while living in India. Due to the continued political tensions in India, Usha's family immigrated to the United States when she was seven years old. Thema Bryant-Davis, a survivor of sexual abuse, witnessed community assault and violence while living in Liberia during the outbreak of a civil war. Throughout her healing, Thema overcame abuse and learned to thrive. In addition, political trauma in our shores wounded our contributors. To illustrate, Patricia Pitta noted that the events of September 11, 2001 traumatized her. She acknowledged that she found a way to cope with such trauma in her faith.

Many of the women psychotherapists recognized the adversity their ancestors encountered and were amazed that such experience did not damage their ancestors' compassion. Such awakening helped them to acknowledge the resilience in the human spirit. As Thema Bryant-Davis reflected: *The struggles we face affect us but do not define us.* Like wounded healers, the contributors' pain functioned as a purifying fire that assisted them to become healers.

Connectedness

The journey of women psychotherapists entails a deepening of their connection to others, to themselves, and to their world. These women's connectedness facilitated their therapeutic development. They displayed their connectedness through their decision to engage in personal therapy (self-connectedness), their relationships with mentors (connection to others), and their coping with gendered experiences (connectedness with the world).

Research findings suggest that most psychotherapists have been in personal psychotherapy (Pope & Tabachnick, 1994). Certainly, the majority of the women in this anthology identified their personal psychotherapy as a transformative event. Beverly Fauman's personal psychoanalysis helped her to cope with the death of her mother, the end of her first marriage, the examination of her identity within a male-dominated world, and her exploration of concerns about motherhood. Beverly concluded that to be effective, women psychotherapists needed to engage in self-knowledge and reflection. While Patricia Pitta credited her many years of psychoanalytic psychotherapy with helping her with professional connections, Janice Crawford praised her personal therapy with developing her capacity to understand and to love.

Jennifer Ruff noted that she gained insight, developed compassion, and grew spiritual optimism during her personal psychotherapy with a "wonderfully warm and empathic" woman therapist. Likewise, Usha Tummala-Narra observed that she found an empathic woman therapist who helped her to break her silence and share personal material that she could not share with her family. Interestingly, Lillian Comas-Díaz chose a feminist Jungian analyst man over an Australian female psychotherapist. Lillian noted that the woman therapist's internalized oppression seemed to interfere with her ability to empathize with Lillian. Cinzia Levalds observed that therapy is a delicate dance, where the therapist must be attentive to her issues, so that when she encounters similarities with her clients, she knows how to navigate them. In general, the contributors found their personal psychotherapy to be beneficial and recommended women therapists to get to know themselves through this process.

Another experience that the women psychotherapists found valuable in their healing development was the presence of mentors. Most contributors identified several mentors in their life. Jennifer Ruff named her mother as an important mentor. When she wanted to imitate Florence Nightingale and become a nurse, her mother urged her to become a doctor instead. In addition to her parents, Usha Tummala-Narra acknowledged several mentors who helped her integrate diverse aspects of her journey as a female healer. In particular, she described a clinical supervisor who told her: "When you are in doubt of what to do [in therapy], be a human being." Moreover, Janice Crawford recognized her teachers, therapists, partners, and clients as important mentors in her life. Succinctly put, most contributors such as Lillian Comas-Díaz, Beverly Fauman, and Beverly Greene, among others, acknowledged mentors who profoundly influenced their role as healers.

The women psychotherapists identified gendered experiences as transformative events in their life. Such experiences helped them in their transition from disconnection into connectedness. The contributors discussed the following gendered experiences: pregnancy, motherhood, and immigration.

Several women identified being pregnant as perhaps the quintessential gendered event in their life and career. Carla Bradshaw exquisitely discussed the impact of her pregnancies on her clients as well as on her role as a therapist. She elaborated on the clinical issues related to the pregnant psychotherapist. Likewise, Beverly Fauman analyzed the effect of her pregnancy on her clinical practice. For example, her supervisors told her that it would be inappropriate to intrude on her patients' fantasies by sharing the news of her pregnancy. Moreover, some of her colleagues were dismissive, and even angry towards her. Beverly coped by writing her patients' reactions to her pregnancy.

Numerous women psychotherapists discussed motherhood and its impact on their lives. Although Patricia Pitta found private practice and mothering to be a good combination because it allowed her to be with her children as they grew up, she felt that there was something missing.

Similarly, Carla Bradshaw recognized the professional opportunities she missed while raising her children. However, she acknowledged that her daughters "raised" her through motherhood. Moreover, Carla revealed that she found a holding community of parents who became close friends.

Other women discussed not becoming a biological mother. For example, Jennifer Ruff risked the possibility of becoming a biological mother when she decided to enter graduate school. Later on she married and became the stepmother of two sons. Along these lines, Lillian Comas-Díaz discussed her decision of not having biological children. Instead, she revealed how she expresses her generativity by nurturing younger generations.

Motherhood and female healing seemed to be related. Indeed, healing from a feminine perspective has been labeled as the professionalization of motherhood (Philipson, 1993). Throughout herstory, female healers have embodied the mythic great mother in their role of protectress, healer, and nurturer (Kerewesky-Halpern, 1995). Notably, Beverly Fauman stated that as a female, many of her clients hear her suggestions as maternal. Moreover, Janice Crawford declared her therapeutic work as a way to honor her mother and every other woman (including herself) as the "creative crucible" of life, whether the woman becomes a biological mother or not. Succinctly put, a female psychotherapist embodies a position as an enlightened mother.

Another gendered event discussed by some psychotherapists was immigration. Immigration tends to affect females differently from males. As indicated before, Usha Tummala-Narra experienced her parents' unequal gender treatment after immigration, limiting her contact with males, while allowing her brother freedom in dating. Usha identified her subsequent cultural adjustments as the hiding of the self and culture. Likewise, Lillian Comas-Díaz recalled how she became an ethnic minority female after her migration, becoming a transcultural woman who heals in a strange land. Similarly, a mixed race woman who moved multiple times and lived in Japan as well as in the United States, Carla Bradshaw described her feelings about being "foreign." Furthermore, several women, such as Janice Crawford, Beverly Fauman, Patricia Pitta, and Marcella Bakur Weiner identified their ancestors' history of immigration as an important factor in their healing development.

Empowerment

Most women bear a legacy of historic subordination and oppression. Likewise, many of the women psychotherapists in this collection experienced sexism, racism, and racist sexism. Paradoxically, such experiences helped to empower them. In the words of Carla Bradshaw, these women refused to be broken. For instance, Beverly Greene asserted that growing up in the midst of racism prepared her to become a therapist. She acknowledged the capacity to heal in the midst of pain as an empowering force in her life.

Numerous contributors experienced gender discrimination in the form of sexual harassment, unequal pay, and sexual abuse. To illustrate, Beverly Fauman reported that she was paid less than her male psychiatrist colleagues during the beginning of her career. Similarly, Jennifer Ruff noted that male staff subjected her to sexist denigrated "jokes" working with prison inmates. Other women psychotherapists experienced additional forms of gender oppression such as misogyny and racist sexism. For example, Usha Tummala-Narra heard Indian women make negative comments about her dark skin color and Lillian Comas-Díaz was called *jabá*—a racial appellation denoting a mixed race female with kinky hair. While discussing racist sexism, Thema Bryant-Davis lamented that she was not trained to deal with clients' comments about her race and gender interaction. Carla Bradshaw credited being a psychotherapist with helping her to understand the difference between what had been her responsibility and what abuse had been perpetrated on her due to the interaction of her gender and race.

The contributors acknowledged the need to empower women due to the female gender status in society. They identified the women's and the civil rights movements as powerful forces in shaping their personal and professional lives. For instance, Janice Crawford recognized that the women's movement helped her to realize how female clients can empower themselves. More specifically, Thema Bryant-Davis affirmed that therapeutic empowerment helps women to choose between "the things they want to release, the things they want to modify, the things they want to keep, and the new things they want to gain." Most of the contributors acknowledged the need to empower themselves. For example, although many recognized the value of nurturing their feminine side, they also realized the need to balance their feminine and masculine aspects in their therapeutic work.

Feminism exerted a major influence on all of the women psychotherapists in this collection. Indeed, several women acknowledged the incorporation of feminist principles into their therapeutic work. Although Beverly Greene revealed that she considers herself a feminist therapist, she acknowledged that historically, feminism did not include all women. Indeed, the women of color in this volume observed that they integrated diverse perspectives into their feminist empowerment approach. To illustrate, Lillian Comas-Díaz reported that she complements feminism with multiculturalism. Similarly, Carla Bradshaw, Patricia Pitta, and Usha Tummala-Narra recognized the influence of multiculturalism in their lives and professional practice.

Thema Bryant-Davis best summarized the women psychotherapists' position on empowerment: "As a female therapist, I have to model for myself, my daughter, and my clients what it means to embody some of the traits that are traditionally described as feminine as well as some of those traditionally associated with masculinity."

Holism

The majority of the contributors endorsed holism in their evolution from woman psychotherapist to female healer. Throughout their journey, the women developed a consciousness as a psychotherapist-healer. This type of consciousness facilitated their use of both intuition and rationality, and helped them to develop a combined feminine and instrumental approach to psychotherapy. In other words, these women learned to heal with their mind and heart. Such *thinking heart* method enhanced their special attunement, a skill that facilitates healing at multiple levels.

As an illustration, Patricia Pitta asserted that she was born with a sensitivity that enabled her to feel others and to be in touch with her feelings. Throughout her journey she learned to use such gift in healing. Several women identified this gift as intuition. Beverly Fauman asserted that the loss of her mother and the end of her first marriage heightened her gift of intuition. To improve her skill, she began a meditation practice and traveled to China, India, and Tibet. Likewise, Lillian Comas-Díaz acknowledged intuition as a therapeutic tool, and studied clinicians' use of intuition in psychotherapy to enrich her gift. Interestingly, in the book *Women's Ways of Knowing*, Mary F. Belenky and her colleagues (1997) identified the biblical "still small voice" or intuition as the voice of God.

Some of the women psychotherapists acknowledged a spiritual component in their healing practice. For instance, Marcella Bakur Weiner commented: "God is in charge." After her mother's death, Cinzia Levalds recognized a connection between the physical body and emotions. As a result, she developed a spiritual focus in her therapeutic work. Notably, Jennifer Ruff provided an illustration of a spiritual component in healing. She shared the spiritual assessment she uses with her clients. Jennifer examines her clients' belief (or lack of) in transcendental deity and their endorsement of a religious or spiritual practice. Additionally, Jennifer explores the impact of her clients' beliefs on their problems, coping, and relationships.

Following a similar line of reasoning, several women psychotherapists discussed their use of energy in their work. Cinzia Levalds observed that she feels her patients' energy interact with her own energy during psychotherapy. Along these lines, she embraced the spiritual principle: what happens to us happens *for* us.

Likewise, Marcella Bakur Weiner disclosed that she uses energy in her psychotherapeutic practice. Moreover, Janice Crawford discussed the effect of *life force field of energy* in her constellation therapy work. She described Bert Hellinger's concept of life force as a representation of the energy of love. Similarly, Cinzia Levalds identified *love* as the energy that heals. Additionally, she advised women psychotherapists against working with anyone they cannot love. To enhance their holistic approach, several of the women reconnected with their cultural and spiritual roots. For example, Usha Tummala-Narra studied the *Bhagavad Gita*, one of the primary holy books of Hinduism. Similarly, Lillian Comas-Díaz reconnected with her folk healing cultural roots.

In summary, the psychotherapist-healers' intuition and sensitivity to their inner voice allow them to hear their clients' inner voice. They are committed to heal and to be healed, or as Lillian Comas-Díaz said: *they assist women to translate their stories of distress into epics of joy*.

Commitment

The women psychotherapist-healers expressed a strong commitment to transforming themselves and their communities. They acknowledged a dedication to being a healing force in the world. As such, these women value empowerment, service, community, and social action. Moreover, they integrate spirituality into their quest for social justice. Within their psychotherapist-healer role they commit to work on women's issues such as sexual abuse, domestic violence, sexual discrimination, sexism, racism, misogyny, and other types of female trauma.

The wisewomen in this anthology demonstrated their inclusiveness as they give back to their communities. Many of these women have a transformative presence in their communities. For example, Patricia Pitta volunteers to charities, psychological groups, and other community organizations, often serving on their boards. Marcella Bakur Weiner is president of a community mental health center in Brooklyn, which caters to and treats the indigent and their families, without charge. Like Patricia and

Marcella, Carla Bradshaw, Thema Bryant-Davis, Lillian Comas-Díaz, Beverly Fauman, Beverly Greene, Jennifer Ruff, and Usha Tummala-Narra are active in their local and national professional organizations. Janice Crawford has volunteered with the New York City National Organization for Women.

The contributors in this anthology *lift other women* as they climb the ladder of life. Beverly Fauman mentors medical students and residents. In this role she advocates for flexible alternatives for the female professionals she trains, supervises, and treats. According to Beverly, this is her version of "paying it forward." Moreover, Thema Bryant-Davis is a spokesperson for the awareness of female trauma. Indeed, these women heal in the midst of social injustice. They work along the side of the oppressed and marginalized. They treat a variety of client populations including children, adolescents, and families, as well as adults, and the elderly. Additionally, they have seen individuals with a wide range of clinical conditions, such as seriously ill (Patricia Pitta), AIDS patients (Janice Crawford), MS patients (Cinzia Levalds), obese clients (Patricia Pitta) chronically ill elderly (Marcella Bakur Weiner), incarcerated males (Patricia Pitta, Jennifer Ruff), trauma survivors (Carla Bradshaw, Thema Bryant-Davis, Lillian Comas-Díaz, Beverly Fauman), immigrants and multicultural individuals (Lillian Comas-Díaz, Beverly Greene, Usha Tummala-Narra, and Patricia Pitta), among many others. Certainly, the work of women healers is transformative and revolutionary (Ehrenreich & English, 1973).

Wisewomen Lessons: Challenges and Blessings

The women in this anthology revealed that if they had to do it again, they would become a psychotherapist. The female qualities of spirituality, namely, intuition, nurturing, and healing permeate the contributors' stories. Such narratives inspire us to follow a female healing path. They alert us of the challenges that many women face in accepting their healer role. According to Elisabeth Brooke (1995), women healers inherit a historical wound due to the torture and execution that silenced women healers accused of being witches from the 15th to the 17th centuries in Europe. To counteract this historical gender wound, Elisabeth Brooke advised women healers to do the best for themselves and their clients, to nurture and be nurtured, to overcome false barriers that exist between them and their clients, to maintain those boundaries that are necessary for self-protection, and to balance material profit with intellectual and emotional productivity.

The women psychotherapist-healers in this collection are living examples of such advice. For example, Thema Bryant-Davis counseled women healers to balance compassion with boundaries and to *press pause* before they burn out. These women also embody the inherent blessings in being a female healer. To illustrate, Patricia Pitta stated that being a psychologist affords her the gift of learning about the stage of life she faces and to cope with the challenges of the journey of life. Indeed, these wisewomen combine the art and science of human transformation. As experts of the thinking heart they offer you their collective wisdom in the following lessons.

Women Psychotherapists' Wisdom

- Honor your clients/patients, their pain, and their stories
- Reconnect with who you are
- Be aware of your wounds, biases, and gifts as a woman
- Know your self and seek healing
- Acknowledge the impostor syndrome
- Invoke your resilience and refuse to be broken
- Connect with others without disconnecting from yourself
- Have friends who are therapists, and have friends who are not
- Prioritize self-care
- Develop your intuition
- Lift as you climb
- Nurture your feminine aspect and exercise your masculine side—in other words, be kind and strong
- Link your past with your present, and envision a future
- Strive to infuse hope and grace into your healing role
- Allow your artistic healer and psychotherapist identities to inform and strengthen each other
- Cultivate your thinking heart
- Become an expert of the heart
- Let love flow into your healing
- Reclaim your psychotherapist-healer self

As you become a psychotherapist-healer, you will find a lost path. Throughout this journey you will be both *healing and healed.*

References

Belenky, M. F., Clinchy, B. M., Golberger, N. R., & Tarule, J. M. (1997). *Women's ways of knowing: The development of self, voice, and mind.* New York: Basic Books.

Brooke, E. (1995). *Woman healers: Portraits of herbalists, physicians and midwives.* Rochester, VT: Healing Arts Press.

Cantor, D. W., ed. (1990). *Women as therapists.* Northvale, NJ: Jason Aronson.

Davis-Kimball, J. (2002). *Warrior women: An archeologist's search for history's hidden heroines.* New York: Warner Books.

Ehrenreich, B., & English, D. (1973). *Witches, midwives and nurses: A history of women healers.* Old Westbury, NY: The Feminist Press.

Kakar, S. (1985). Psychoanalysis and non-Western cultures. *International Review of Psychoanalysis, 12,* 441–448.

Kerewesky-Halpern, B. (1995). Healing with mother metaphors: Serbian conjurers word magic. In C. S. McClain (Ed.) *Women as healers: Cross cultural perspectives* (pp. 115–125). New Brunswick, NJ: Rutgers University Press.

Padilla-Walker, L., Harper, J., & Jensen, A. (2010). Self-regulation as a mediator between sibling relationship quality and early adolescents' positive and negative outcomes. *Journal of Family Psychology, 21*(4), 419–428.

Philipson, I. J. (1993). *On the shoulders of women: The feminization of psychotherapy.* New York: Guilford Press.

Pope, K., & Tabachnick, B. G. (1994). Therapists as patients: A national survey of psychologists' experiences, problems, and beliefs. *Professional Psychology: Research and Practice. 25*(3), 247–258.

Tisdell, E. J. (2002). Spiritual development and cultural context in the lives of women adult educators for social change. *Journal of Adult Development, 9*(2), 127–140.

Index

Contributors

Carla Bradshaw, Ph.D., is a clinical psychologist in the Seattle, Washington, area in the northwestern United States. She has 27 years in clinical private practice and also provides supervision to early career psychologists and graduate students in clinical psychology. She is published in the areas of multiracial experience, multiracial identity development, and culturally competent psychotherapy. Carla is also active in the state and national psychological associations on behalf of ethnic minority psychologists.

Thema Bryant-Davis, Ph.D., is an associate professor of psychology and Director of the Culture and Trauma Research Lab at Pepperdine University. She was the 2010–2011 president of the Society for the Psychology of Women. Dr. Bryant-Davis is a licensed clinical psychologist with expertise in assisting diverse trauma survivors on the path to healing and empowerment. She is the author of *Thriving in the Wake of Trauma: A Multicultural Guide*. A former psychology representative to the United Nations, Dr. Bryant-Davis is co-author of the American Psychological Association's resolution against racism and racial discrimination. She has provided trainings on trauma psychology, culture, and self-care for schools, prisons, churches, medical centers, universities, police officers, judges, mental health professionals, and community members, nationally and globally.

Lillian Comas-Díaz is a clinical psychologist in private practice in Washington, D.C., the executive director of the Transcultural Mental Health Institute, and a clinical professor at the George Washington University School of Medicine. The former director of the American Psychological

Association's Office of Ethnic Minority Affairs, Dr. Comas-Díaz was a faculty member at the Yale University Department of Psychiatry, where she directed its Hispanic Clinic. She has been a member of fact-finding mental health delegations to Chile, South Africa, the former Soviet Union, Eastern Europe, India, Nepal, China, and Tibet. The author of more than a hundred publications, Dr. Comas-Diaz's writings focus on women's issues, culture, spirituality, ethnicity, social class, and creativity.

Janice Crawford, LCSW, SEP, is a trauma specialist in private practice in New York City. She also provides training for clinicians in present and multi-generational trauma treatment and is on the faculty of the Hellinger Learning Center.

Beverly Fauman, MD, is an associate professor in the Department of Psychiatry at the University of Michigan, where she directs the mental health program for the health officers (interns, residents, and fellows) at the University of Michigan Health System. She also sees students ranging from 16-year-old freshmen to graduate students in their 50s and 60s.

Beverly Greene, Ph.D. and ABBP, received a doctorate from Adelphi University, worked in public mental health for 10 years, and then joined the faculty of St. John's University and became a professor of psychology. A practicing psychologist in New York City, she is a fellow of the APA Divisions 9, 12, 29, 35, 42, 44, and 45, a diplomate in clinical psychology on the American Board of Professional Psychology, and a fellow of the Academy of Clinical Psychology. Recipient of nine national awards for publications deemed outstanding contributions to the psychological literature, she has focused on women of color, lesbians, African Americans, the interactions of race, gender, sexual orientation, and other identities in relation to development and the psychotherapy process.

Cinzia Levalds, M.A. and Ph.D., earned her master's degree from Southern Methodist University, where she graduated summa cum laude and with departmental distinction in psychology. She earned her Ph.D. from the University of Texas Southwestern Medical School. She has a private practice in Texas, where she conducts assessments and psychotherapy and has worked in conjunction with UTSW as a supervisor to graduate students in the Department of Clinical Psychology, and has participated as part of the faculty who conducted training for the Multiple Sclerosis Comprehensive Treatment Program at UTSW.

Patricia Pitta, Ph.D., is a Clinical Board–Certified Family-Couple Psychologist and an approved supervisor of the American Association of Marriage and Family Therapy, practicing in Manhasset, New York. She has been an adjunct professor and supervisor at St. John's University for 20 years. She specializes in treatment of individuals, children, adolescents, and couples. Her areas of expertise are anxiety, depression, family interaction processes, and patterns throughout the life cycle. She envisions a client's dilemma from an integrated perspective of the individual's contribution as well as the family's and larger system's contribution to the creation and maintenance of the dilemma. All dilemmas can be solved if you do the work to promote and make changes.

Jennifer Ruff, Ph.D., is a clinical psychologist in the California Department of Corrections and Rehabilitation, where she specializes in chronic pain treatment. She is also clinical faculty at the University of California, San Francisco's Department of Family and Community Medicine residency program.

Pratyusha Tummala-Narra, Ph.D., is an assistant professor in the Department of Counseling, Developmental, and Educational Psychology at Boston College and a teaching associate at Cambridge Health Alliance/ Harvard Medical School. Her scholarly interests include immigration, trauma, and psychodynamic psychotherapy.

Marcella Bakur Weiner, Ph.D., a fellow of the APA, also has a doctorate in metaphysics/theology. A former senior research scientist for New York State Department of Mental Hygiene and an adjunct professor at Columbia University's Department of Psychology, she is currently president of the advisory council of Mapleton-Midwood Community Mental Health Center. As faculty for the International Association of Human Relations, Dr. Weiner has conducted training for professionals in countries such as Egypt, Thailand, Israel, Sweden, Japan, England, and Turkey. Author of 23 books and 75 articles, one of her most recent books is *Psychotherapy and Religion: Many Paths, One Journey*. She practices in Brooklyn and New York City.

www.ingramcontent.com/pod-product-compliance
Ingram Content Group UK Ltd.
Pitfield, Milton Keynes, MK11 3LW, UK
UKHW012041150926
475560UK00001B/117

9 780765 707871